The
SNARLING
LOGICIAN

The
SNARLING
LOGICIAN

Reflections on Reason, Rationalization, and Religious Belief

ANDREW MARKER

iUniverse®

THE SNARLING LOGICIAN
REFLECTIONS ON REASON, RATIONALIZATION, AND RELIGIOUS BELIEF

iUniverse books may be ordered through booksellers or by contacting:

iUniverse
1663 Liberty Drive
Bloomington, IN 47403
www.iuniverse.com
1-800-Authors (1-800-288-4677)

ISBN: 978-1-4917-5111-4 (sc)
ISBN: 978-1-4917-5112-1 (e)

Library of Congress Control Number: 2014918969

Printed in the United States of America.

iUniverse rev. date: 10/17/2014

I do not think myself any further concerned for the success of what I have written, than as it is agreeable to truth.

—George Berkeley, *Principles of Human Knowledge*

CONTENTS

INTRODUCTION: OF BOOKS

1

As incredibly difficult as it might be to achieve for oneself any real understanding of things, it is harder still to get other people to understand. Communication is inevitably partial. Our foes misunderstand us on purpose, our friends by accident. Even our friends sometimes comprehend only half of what we have written. They then fill in the rest with plausible guesses together with reflections of their own. The resulting interpretation may not be exactly what we had in mind, but it is no worse, and often represents an improvement. Their sympathy with our aims leads them to attribute to us a sagacity we never possessed but had only groped toward. Foes, on the other hand, seem to apply a principle of malice rather than one of charity. The half they do not understand gets filled not with sense but with nonsense. This permits them to manufacture an opponent of straw, or, as I prefer to call it, a "were-dunce"—that is, an opponent who is half man, half moron. How many scholarly debates have raged over these fictitious monsters, the were-dunces?

An author can protect himself in three ways. The first is to write clearly, since plain language is less likely to be misinterpreted. The second is to think clearly. No one can understand an author who does not understand himself. Finally, an author must have something important to say. The gravity of the message encourages the audience to read his text more than once. Repeated readings help to close the gap in comprehension so that the half that is understood becomes three-quarters, and then seven-eighths.

I cannot tell how well I have done by any of these three measures. Personal bias prevents me from having a rational perspective on my own work. I can say that I have been wrestling with philosophical problems for more than thirty-five years. Just as the elements within a steel alloy eventually fall into the right order if the metal is repeatedly heated and cooled, so it has been with my thoughts. After countless cycles of reading, reflection, and attempts at writing, they have finally fallen into what seems like the right order. I have presented them here to the best of my ability. If the few insights contained in this volume seem scant payment for the reader's time and trouble, they nonetheless represent all I had to offer. Should my purported "insights" turn out to be delusions, then I apologize for that in advance. On the other hand, I might very reasonably insist, as Nietzsche once did, that "if this book is incomprehensible to anyone and jars on his ears, the fault, it seems to me, is not necessarily mine." An author can only do so much. After that, the burden falls upon his audience to read slowly, cautiously, and with circumspection.[i]

It might be suspected that the issues of philosophy, though no doubt important in themselves, have already been discussed so thoroughly that nothing of any value remains to be said about them. I cannot believe this to be true. Had everything to be done in philosophy been done already, then why are we not all wise? As long as folly fills the world, philosophers will have work to do. There must be discoveries in the field as yet unmade, terrain still unexplored, and insights not yet grasped. We cannot find any of these things unless we keep looking for them, and looking, and looking …

2

In 1713 the English Deist Anthony Collins, a friend of John Locke's, published *A Discourse on Free-Thinking* in which he defined his subject matter as follows:

> By free-thinking I mean the use of the understanding in endeavoring to find out the meaning of any proposition whatsoever, in considering the nature of the evidence for or against it, and in judging of it according to the seeming force or weakness of the evidence.[ii]

Freethinkers are called such because they have thrown off the shackles of faith. Yet to be a freethinker does not mean that one thinks without constraints. On the contrary, freethinking implies a voluntary submission to the rule of reason. For a freethinker, reason has a magisterial function; it is the final arbiter of truth and falsity. He therefore makes a commitment to follow reason wherever it leads, with no guarantee that it will lead him to any particular destination. The freethinker cannot know in advance whether his inquiries will conduct him to the truth; nor can he possibly know what the truth will turn out to be. Still, the freethinker is willing to live with this double uncertainty. To embrace a measure of perpetual doubt is a part of the commitment he makes. Also involved in that commitment is a determination to go by the evidence. The rules of reason, after all, just are rules for the proper treatment of evidence: how to collect it, interpret it, and make inferences from it. The freethinker's freedom means nothing unless he adheres to these rules, which he takes to be universally valid laws of thought. His freedom is thus a freedom constrained within the rule of law. His independence is married to a demand for self-discipline.

The freethinker's attitude stands opposed to that taken by persons of faith, no matter what faith might be involved. In matters of faith, the faithful grant to reason not a magisterial but only a ministerial role. They thus compel reason to be the apologist and defense attorney of their dogma. The faithful believe they can bring faith into harmony with reason. A freethinker, though, will see the "harmony" so imposed as both a corruption of reason and a betrayal of it. Faith, he will insist, is a terrible thing to do to a mind. In his view, the whole process called "faith seeking understanding" represents not philosophy but mere philodoxy—which is to say it is the love not of truth but of one's own preordained conclusions.

Freethinkers have not always received a warm welcome in the world. In the old days we were persecuted, tortured, or killed, and our books were burned. Although such overt violence has become less common, the hostility that produced it remains. Expressions of it have merely become more subtle. Consider what the noted philosopher Roger Scruton had to say regarding J. L. Mackie's famous work, *The Miracle of Theism*: "a useful book by a man who spent much of his life lecturing God on His non-existence, and who is now being lectured in his turn." Although Scruton probably thought this remark very clever, to an atheist it sounds like a cheap shot taken at a distinguished scholar. Apparently Scruton believed that God has reserved a special place in hell for unbelievers who have the audacity to defend their views in public. There a just and merciful God torments [former] atheists with endless harangues about how wrong they were. Such hatefulness and narrow-minded bigotry, so casually expressed, reveals the seamy underside of Scruton's religion of love.[iii]

Immanuel Kant found irreligious authors even more useful than did Scruton, and he treated them with much greater tolerance:

> When I hear that the freedom of the will, the hope of a future life, and the existence of God have been overthrown by the arguments of some able writer, I feel a strong desire to read his book; for I expect that he will add to my knowledge, and impart greater clearness and distinctness to my views by the argumentative power shown in his writings. But I am perfectly certain, even before I have opened the book, that he has not succeeded in a single point, not because I believe I am in possession of irrefutable demonstrations of these important propositions, but because this transcendental critique, which has disclosed to me the power and limits of pure reason, has fully convinced me that, as it is insufficient to establish the affirmative, it is as powerless, and even more so, to assure us of the truth of the negative answer to these questions.[iv]

Kant's willingness, even eagerness, to read the works of his opponents is laudable. I can only hope that my Christian and Jewish contemporaries will be so open-minded. Yet the open-mindedness Kant displays in the first sentence of this passage seems tarnished by the utter close-mindedness of the second sentence. How can Kant be so sure that his opponents are wrong and that their arguments are futile? Even if the arguments he presents in the *Critique of Pure Reason* were cogent, they could hardly warrant the perfect certainty Kant claims to possess. There is scarcely any proposition in philosophy so well established as that.

Kant explains himself about forty pages further on:

> I am irresistibly constrained to believe in the existence of God and in a future life; and I am sure that nothing can make me waver in this belief, since I should thereby overthrow my moral maxims, the renunciation of which would render me hateful in my own eyes.[v]

Kant believed this entitled him to regard the arguments of skeptics in roughly the same way that physicists regard the blueprints drawn up by those who claim to have invented perpetual motion machines.

I think Kant was wrong on multiple counts. Reason is not so impotent as he imagined. That it cannot demonstrably prove either the existence or nonexistence of God in no way suggests that it cannot determine which belief is the more reasonable one to hold. However, if reason were to leave the issue perfectly in balance, with no firm answer one way or another, why should that result not produce in us a perfect agnosticism? And how could it ever justify a leap of faith into religious belief? Kant's view that belief in God and an afterlife is required as a prop to morality is undermined by his own words. Were we to renounce morality, he says, we would become hateful in our own eyes. On that point he is absolutely correct. What follows from that point, though, is a conclusion directly opposite to the one Kant tries to draw. Suppose for a moment that there is no God and no afterlife either. In that case we would still wish to retain our ethics, not because God commands us to, nor because of any rewards or punishments involved, but simply because deep down each of us does in fact wish to be the kind of person who deserves the love we instinctively lavish on ourselves. The desire to survive critical self-examination is the ultimate ground and motivation for moral behavior and is quite independent of any theological trappings. Morality, then, needs no support from religion, and Kant's fear, that he could not have the one without the other, seems to have been entirely unfounded.

Kant would complain that to remove God from the picture is to remove morality's obligatory aspect. He is right. The moral law differs from positive law in precisely that respect. The positive laws decreed by men or by gods enjoy obligatory force in proportion to the legislator's power to enforce his decrees. The rules of morality are not like that; they are more like the rules of reason. As with the principles of logic or the canons of epistemology, moral rules are not our invention. For the most part they just are what they are, though sometimes with room left for interpretation. We cannot avoid any of these rules entirely, since they belong to the very fabric of our nature. Yet a full commitment to them must be voluntary. A sovereign can compel us to obey positive law, but no one can literally compel us to be moral, any more than they can compel us to respect *modus ponens*, or Occam's razor. This view of morality deprives it of nothing essential. If anything, it only serves to augment the dignity of moral endeavors.

As for myself, I do not believe either in God or in the immortality of the human soul. I do believe there is something that deserves to be called freedom of the will, even though the nature of it may be somewhat less exalted than is often supposed. Since I think that I will cease to be when I die, I do fear death. However, I am not afraid of that fear. It is a normal part of human life. I feel no impulse to try to lessen it through the adoption of more comforting beliefs. This tranquility in the face of my own perpetual doubts and fears opens the way for me to pursue free thought as a way of life.

3

The Snarling Logician is a sequel to my first book, *The Ladder.* The two works appear to me to be entirely consistent with each other. The same world view appears in each. There is some overlap of material. Both books contain reflections on the philosophic quest, and both argue against the existence of God. The chief difference between them is that *The Snarling Logician* focuses on epistemological questions relating to the concept of belief, while *The Ladder* was centered on more purely logical issues connected to the concept of truth.

In *The Ladder* I argued against the correspondence theory of truth. According to that theory, truth consists in saying that what is, is, and that what is not, is not. Yet not all statements to which we attribute truth values concern what is or is not the case. Many involve assertions about what should be, could be, or would be the case. These do not fit neatly into the correspondence mold. To what are moral truths supposed to correspond? How would it even be possible for true counterfactual statements to correspond to anything? What about mathematical truths involving complex and imaginary numbers? Do they have to correspond to something, and what if they don't? To respect the diversity of truths, while also honoring our very powerful common sense intuition that there is some essential link between truth and reality, I proposed the containment theory of truth. Containment theory employs a possible worlds model both for interpreting the content of propositions and for distinguishing true propositions from false ones. Among its other merits, the theory provides a very natural way to deal with logical paradoxes, without placing any arbitrary limitations on what does or does not count as a class.

I still believe that containment theory represents the right solution to the problems it addressed. I cannot improve on what I said about it in *The Ladder*, so I must refer the reader to that earlier work for the details. However, a knowledge of *The Ladder* is not required for an understanding of *The Snarling Logician*. In fact, I would prefer that everyone read *The Snarling Logician* first, since it is the better of the two.

THE QUEST FOR WISDOM

Section 1

THE GAME

As a boy I played a game that consisted of a wooden box with a built-in board. The board could be tilted left, right, forward, or backward using plastic knobs placed along the sides of the box. The board's surface contained a labyrinth, at every turn of which was a hole. I think there were about sixty such holes. The idea was to use the knobs to maneuver a small steel ball through the labyrinth without letting it drop into a hole. If the ball dropped, play had to start over, from the beginning. The game took more skill than I could muster. Even after much practice, I could never complete the course. My ball always fell in a hole.

Doing philosophy is a lot like playing that game. The intellectual landscape of philosophy consists of innumerable puzzles, problems, and mysteries, all related to one another by a complex network of logical interconnections. Philosophers must try to navigate through the resulting maze without succumbing to any of the hidden pitfalls. But philosophy is infinitely more difficult than that children's game. Players of the game can see when their balls have disappeared into holes. A philosopher, on the other hand, does not immediately know when he has erred. He may fall into a "hole," decide he likes it there, and make himself to home. The hole becomes his fort. He builds walls around it; he arms himself to defend it at all costs. He calls the hole his "considered position." He proudly believes himself to have arrived at reflective equilibrium. All that means is that he cannot get out of his hole.

To write philosophy is to give the reader directions to one's hole. A philosopher who had conquered the entire maze of his subject could presumably teach others how to do likewise. Unfortunately there is no good reason to think that anyone has achieved such a triumph. The maze, as far as I know, has never been navigated without error, nor has any accurate map of its pitfalls ever been drawn. The most any philosopher can do is humbly to set up sign posts to mark the holes he has already sidestepped, so that readers may advance at least as far through the labyrinth as has the philosopher himself.

Sign posts, as Wittgenstein observed, can always be misread. One can interpret them in different ways. The philosopher who records his alleged wisdom for posterity must therefore trust his reader's judgment. He must assume that his audience will display enough diligence, and have sufficient common sense, to figure out which way his signs point.

Sign posts are symbolic tools. A prosthetic arm is also a kind of tool. To give someone a prosthetic arm is to presume that he or she lacks something, namely, a real arm. The prosthesis is meant to remedy that defect. No such presumption of deficiency is involved if you give someone a sword. The gift of a sword actually requires the contrary assumption, that the recipient's arm works just fine. The sword is intended to augment the striking power of that healthy limb. A philosopher's sign posts are more like swords than prosthetic limbs; they are meant not to replace the reader's natural intellectual abilities but only to enhance the force with which the reader might deploy them.

How can the philosopher place so much trust in his readers, given that many of them will likely misuse or despise his so-called "gift," and that many others will insult him by turning his words into those of a were-dunce? Well, I did not say that such trust is always deserved, only that it is always necessary.

Section 2

THE AUDIENCE

Doing philosophy is a solitary affair. The philosopher puts no one's ball at risk but his own. He must tilt his board himself, working the knobs without help. His conclusions belong to him alone; he is responsible for them. If he falls in a hole, it becomes his hole. He owns it. He need not answer to any authority higher than that of his own intellectual conscience.

Writing philosophy is a public event. When a philosopher puts pen to paper, he becomes a political animal. It is the reader's ball that concerns him. Yet the public to whom the philosopher addresses his words is inevitably a small one. He must write for the few, because while the need for wisdom may be great, the demand for it is not. This cadre of receptive minds may, however, include amateurs as well as professionals in the field. "Philosophy," as Mortimer Adler used to say, "is everybody's business." By this he meant not that everybody does philosophize but that everybody can, and everyone ought to. Philosophy is a democratic discipline, open to all, the only entrance requirements being an open mind and a love of something we fondly call "wisdom."

The reader might well wonder whether this love is not always unrequited. "Philosophy seems a vain endeavor," the reader might say. "For to read philosophy, and to write it, are, according to you, nothing more than the giving and receiving of directions to a hole! And are holes not defined by their errors?" To this I can only say that some holes are better than others. Errors can be more or less egregious. A philosopher provides an important public service if he can help even a tiny number of readers escape their holes and proceed to others more advanced. What makes this service important? Just this, that while the demand for wisdom may not be great, the need for it is.

Section 3

GOOD SENSE

In philosophy, opinions may be true or false, insightful or ignorant, but method is everything. Method is destiny, because method dictates results. Aim a rifle in the wrong direction, and the target will be missed, no matter what make or model of weapon one uses. Given poor aim, a larger bore only increases the potential for disaster downrange, for if the target is not hit, something else will be. Intelligence is like a rifle: when handled carelessly, it does harm in proportion to its caliber. Proper method is what ensures that one's intelligence will get pointed the right way. Descartes understood this principle, as the opening paragraph of his *Discourse on Method* shows:

> For to be possessed of a vigorous mind is not enough; the prime requisite is rightly to apply it. The greatest minds, as they are capable of the highest excellences, are open likewise to the greatest aberrations; and those who travel very slowly may yet make far greater progress, provided they keep always to the straight road, than those who, while they run, forsake it.[vi]

Unfortunately, this insight follows upon the heels of a thoughtless prejudice:

> Good sense is, of all things among men, the most equally distributed; for everyone thinks himself so abundantly provided with it, that those even that are the most difficult to satisfy in everything else, do not usually desire a larger measure of this quality than they already possess. And it is not likely that all are mistaken: the conviction is rather to be held as testifying that the power of judging aright and of distinguishing truth from error, which is properly what is called good sense or reason, is by nature equal in all men.[vii]

Perhaps Descartes is right on the psychological point, that men typically do think themselves adequately endowed with "good sense or reason." Most men probably think themselves good in bed and handy with their fists; that does not make it so. Distinguishing truth from error is no easy task. Any examination of either books or people should reveal that some of us are more prone to falsity of belief than others. Widespread complacency on this issue would, however, explain why wisdom is not any more plentiful than it seems to be. Men will not get better at the discernment of truth until they come to realize that they are not currently so adept at it as they would wish.

It seems that Descartes has been duped by Plato. In Plato's dialogue the *Meno*, Socrates gets Meno to agree that all bees are alike in beehood. Whatever constitutes the essence of beeness must be possessed equally by all bees. Descartes explicitly endorses this brand of essentialism in the very next paragraph of the *Discourse*:

> I am disposed ... to adopt the common opinion
> of philosophers, who say that the difference
> of greater and less holds only among the
> *accidents*, and not among the *forms*, or natures
> of individuals of the same species.[viii]

Good sense or reason is thought to belong to the form of
humanity, and hence, by this logic, cannot vary among men. All
other qualities, such as memory or imagination, belong among
humanity's accidents, and so may vary as widely as you please.

This will not do. Though I have never become personally
acquainted with any of Plato's Forms, I would hazard the guess
that swimming inheres within the form of fish. Does it follow
that a minnow can swim as fast and as far as a shark? I think
not. By the same token, our common possession of reason does
not entail that we are all equally good at reasoning. It does not
entail that we are all equally good at anything. Human abilities
are subject to individual differences along every dimension, be
that dimension essential to our nature or not.

Having some measure of skill at reasoning is a prerequisite
for philosophy. That we and our readers enjoy this measure is the
best operating assumption for writing philosophy. Yet improving
our skill is always possible and ought to be among the primary
goals of doing philosophy. If the possession of good sense is
considered distinctively human, then so too should be the striving
for better sense. This striving for better sense is what the love of
wisdom is all about.

Section 4

TIME

When writing philosophy, it is best to put several months, even a year or more, between the rough draft and the final copy. Such a long writing sabbatical is required to let one's thoughts ripen. With the passage of time the rough draft will come to look different and feel different. Upon revision the book becomes, you might say, a collaboration between its author and a younger version of himself. The vigor of the youthful self, evident in the rough draft, gets preserved, while the mature judgment of the older thinker recasts the text to make its theses more defensible. Such collaboration reduces, but cannot eliminate, the number of occasions upon which an author must look back at his work and say to himself, "Wow! If only I had not said *that*!"

Reading a text, really reading it and not merely letting its words wash across one's eyeballs, also takes time. How much depends upon both author and reader. The less the two agree on things, the more time it takes for the latter to decipher the former. If an author lives inside a weltanschauung radically opposed to our own, he almost seems to speak a foreign language. Mastering that language is hard work. We have to puzzle out first what that author said, then what he meant, and, finally, what he saw. It requires an imaginative leap to grasp how the world must have looked through his eyes. The payoff for all this effort can be considerable. Authors with whom we disagree are the only ones who can show us the way out of our holes. But even if it is they, not we, who are in the wrong, still they are useful to us. Sometimes the best way to discover a hole is to watch what happens when others fall into it.

Section 5

PAPER BRIDGES

I was in the coffee shop during my freshman year at Saint John's College when I overheard one of the sophomores explain to another freshman the difference between philosophers and engineers. He said that "a philosopher, when confronted with any object, wants to know if it is good; an engineer only asks if it works." These words were spoken with a truly sophomoric air of superiority. This fellow thought himself quite the philosopher. His mind thus dwelt on a plane far above the amoral and merely utilitarian concerns of engineering students. Arthur Schopenhauer, whose mind may have operated on a plane even higher than that sophomore's, expressed similar sentiments about scientists:

> Two Chinamen visiting Europe went to the theater for the first time. One of them occupied himself with trying to understand the theatrical machinery, which he succeeded in doing. The other, despite his ignorance of the language, sought to unravel the meaning of the play. The former is like the astronomer, the latter the philosopher.[ix]

Whenever Western philosophers wish to refer to a language unintelligible to them, they always single out Chinese. I do not know why. Do people in China refer to English or German with the same degree of bafflement?

In *World as Will and Representation*, Schopenhauer often refers to great artists as "geniuses." Artists, he believed, portray in their works the true inner meaning of things. They find the universal in the particular, and so permit us a fleeting glimpse of Plato's abstract Forms. This makes artists and philosophers kindred spirits. I do not recall Schopenhauer ever describing scientists as geniuses. It would be a grudging concession if he did. To Schopenhauer, scientists were mere mechanics. Their work was of a menial type. It belonged to a lower order than that done by artists and philosophers. Like that sophomore, Schopenhauer looked down on scientists as if from a higher plane.

Schopenhauer does capture an important truth. Philosophers really are trying to accomplish a task far more difficult than the one performed by their scientific colleagues. But this hardly gives philosophers any claim to superiority; it simply means that ingenious scientists succeed far more often than do even the most brilliant philosophers. The former do an admirable job of figuring out how the machinery of the cosmic play works. The latter find that the meaning of the play keeps eluding them. It would appear, then, that astronomers are better at astronomy than philosophers are at philosophizing. The higher failure rate among philosophers, which suggests a lower relative competency, should be a source of shame for them, not pride.

Countless errors in philosophy could be avoided if philosophers got into the habit of asking the engineers' question: "Does it work?" The concepts with which philosophers deal are artifacts in exactly the same sense in which bridges and jet aircraft are. Concepts, in other words, are human constructs with a multitude of parts that can work more or less well together. Many of the conceptual structures that philosophers fabricate are like paper bridges. A paper bridge may look beautiful when viewed from certain favored angles, but it is sure to collapse as soon as a truck tries to roll across. Similarly do the elegant constructs of philosophers frequently disintegrate when exposed to the slightest criticism.

No one illustrates the principle just enunciated better than Schopenhauer himself. To read any of his works is to come away impressed with the idea that one has been in the presence of a powerful mind. Schopenhauer's prose style was impeccable. His sense of order produced books that can only be described as tightly organized masterpieces. The metaphysical system he built has an austere beauty to it, unrivaled elsewhere in the history of philosophy. Yet that system fails the engineering test—and fails it miserably.

Schopenhauer explained all the world's phenomena according to the operation of a single restlessly striving, impersonal Will. This Will came in various grades. Its highest form occurred in man; its lowest could be seen in the way a heavy stone presses against the earth with the force of gravity. That the will of a man and the "will" of a stone should be merely different grades of some one thing must seem like so much poetic fancy. Schopenhauer, though, mistook this fancy for a profound metaphysical insight. Of course, he insisted that when he attributed the fall of a rock, the movements of planets, and the growth of plants to the operation of a Will, he meant nothing anthropomorphic by that. It just seemed fitting to him that the force at the heart of all Being should be named after its loftiest manifestation.

But why should the choice of names matter? If Schopenhauer was right in thinking his system free of anthropomorphism, then the term "Will," with its all-too-human connotations, should be inessential. Schopenhauer could just as easily have named the essence of the cosmos after its lowest common denominator. In fact, one could argue that this approach ought to make even more sense. When considering a whole class of phenomena, it is what they all have in common that matters most. Features peculiar to certain favorite members of the class can and should be put aside.

Suppose then we perform the following thought experiment: let us remove the word "Will" from Schopenhauer's books and substitute the term "Gravity." Imagine Schopenhauer declaring Gravity to be the foundation of existence, and imagine him telling us that the inner core of a man is nothing more than gravity, albeit gravity of an especially wonderful type—intellectualized gravity, if you will. Would it not instantly become obvious that Schopenhauer was talking nonsense?

The appeal of Schopenhauer's metaphysic depends on its thinly veiled attempt to humanize the world. We like the idea of finding ourselves in nonhuman nature. It allows us to pretend that man truly is, as Pythagoras put it, "the measure of all things." Our inclinations thus lend an air of plausibility to Schopenhauer's theory of Will. But look what happens when we remove that thin veil. Substituting "Gravity" for "Will" does not alter the logically relevant properties of Schopenhauer's theory. It merely shows us that same theory from another angle. Seen from that perspective, the theory no longer seems to humanize nature; instead it dehumanizes people. Suddenly the appeal of Schopenhauer's metaphysic is gone, and with it, all of that metaphysic's plausibility. The absurdity of the system is exposed.

Schopenhauer never saw this because he let his own words deceive him. He made himself the victim of what Wittgenstein called "the bewitchment of thought by means of language." The philosophical project to which he devoted his entire adult life was thus based on a piece of verbal trickery.

Section 6

DIAGRAMS

Every proof in Euclid's *Elements* comes with a diagram, a constellation of figures, lines, and angles, which appears above, below, or off to the side of the proof. Each step of a proof refers to the attending diagram. Yet the proofs are not about the diagrams. In fact, the diagrams are logically superfluous. Euclid employs them merely as a convenient visual aid to illustrate his geometric theorems. Every theorem is in principle applicable to a potentially infinite number of diagrams. Any diagram meeting certain purely logical criteria will fall under a given theorem's umbrella.

Philosophers enjoy critiquing each other's works. Part of the fun of philosophy consists in picking apart the arguments of one's rivals. Of course, we do this in an altruistic spirit. We want to help our colleagues avoid holes. As a T-shirt once proclaimed, "I am not judgmental—I am merely unselfish with my knowledge of what you are doing wrong!" We philosophers are a very unselfish bunch. However, in refuting some particular author we should never be concerned with that author alone. The errors found in one author may also lurk in the minds of many other thinkers. Each book upon which we comment should therefore be, as it were, the diagram appended to our argument. We should use the book to illustrate some point of general concern, and to expose some common or perennially tempting fallacy. We thus achieve a certain economy of effort, for by refuting one author, we indirectly refute a thousand others who fall under the same umbrella.

Section 7

TRANSPARENCY

In the preface to *The Metaphysics of Mind*, Anthony Kenny acknowledges his indebtedness to both Ludwig Wittgenstein and Gilbert Ryle. Kenny saw these two men as approaching essentially the same goals from different directions. He confesses that he structured his own volume on the pattern provided by Ryle's classic, *The Concept of Mind*. Still, Kenny seems to have thought much more highly of Wittgenstein's methods:

> I came to realize that the ideas which were expressed with crudity as well as vivacity by Ryle had been developed more painfully and more subtly by the much greater genius of Wittgenstein.[x]

Kenny was Ryle's friend, so he would be in a better position than I to judge of Ryle's intelligence. Yet it is not obvious to me, having read both authors, that Wittgenstein was the smarter man. I consider myself admirers of both. It seems to me likely that Kenny was taken in by a certain kind of illusion, an illusion created by these authors' dramatic stylistic differences.

An author is transparent if he announces his objectives at the beginning, spells out his positions clearly, makes his definitions and assumptions explicit, and fills in the steps of his arguments so that nothing is left out. A transparent author leaves little room for rival interpretations of his work. The passages he writes almost interpret themselves, because there is so little doubt as to what propositions the author intends to express. Philosophers who wish to become wise, and to help make others so, should strive for such transparency. It is how philosophy ought to be done. Yet transparency has its drawbacks. To reveal one's thoughts to the world is to reveal them, warts and all. The mistakes one makes become, to the reader at any rate, quite glaring. The philosopher who dares to be this lucid thus risks being thought less intelligent than he is. The reader comes to think herself wiser than that philosopher, precisely because she can so easily see where the philosopher has erred. "How foolish of him not to have caught that gaffe!" the reader muses, again and again. A more enigmatic style, on the other hand, impresses the reader with an appearance of great wisdom. The reader struggles to discern what profound insights the philosopher might be harboring. She fills in all the blanks with reflections of her own, then credits the philosopher with having brilliantly anticipated those views. The reader finds herself inside the philosopher's words, and of course likes what she sees.

Ryle's *Concept of Mind* is far more transparent than Wittgenstein's *Philosophical Investigations*. While this makes Ryle the better role model for future generations of authors, it cost him something in the reputation department. Wittgenstein's manner of attacking problems along indirect pathways encourages readers to think for themselves, which is great, but readers who generously confuse the thoughts he inspires with the thoughts that actually passed through his head will come away with an exaggerated opinion of his brilliance.

Section 8

PRETTY WORDS

Philosophers construct elaborate conceptual edifices in and around their holes. Although they intend these edifices to be impregnable forts, their deaths often leave the parapets unmanned, and so the "forts" quickly become mere museums dedicated to the history of philosophy. Yet even after the superstructures become obsolete, the bricks from which they were made retain their value. Future generations of philosophers will gratefully recycle the insights contained in those bricks.

Nietzsche was an indifferent conceptual architect. His ideas about the overman and the eternal recurrence, so central to his philosophy, would be difficult to defend today. As a brick maker, however, he was brilliant. Individual passages of his frequently sparkle with insight. One of my favorites comes from *Daybreak*. As soon as I read it, I wrote in the margins that by itself the passage justified the whole cost of the book:

> The need for little deviant acts—Sometimes to act *against* one's better judgment when it comes to questions of *custom*; to give way in practice while keeping one's reservations to oneself; to do as everyone else does and thus to show them consideration as it were in compensation

for our deviant opinions: — many tolerably free-minded people regard this, not merely as unobjectionable, but as "honest," "humane," "tolerant," "not being pedantic," and whatever else those pretty words may be with which the intellectual conscience is lulled to sleep: and thus this person takes his child for Christian baptism though he is an atheist; and that person serves in the army as all the world does, however much he may execrate hatred between nations; and a third marries his wife in church because her relatives are pious and is not ashamed to repeat vows before a priest. "It doesn't *really matter* if people like us also do what everyone does and always has done"—this is the thoughtless *prejudice*! The *thoughtless* error! For nothing *matters more* than that an already mighty, anciently established, and irrationally recognized custom should be once more confirmed by a person recognized as rational: it thereby acquires in the eyes of all who come to hear of it the sanction of rationality itself! All respect to your opinions! But little deviant acts are worth more![xi]

Philosophers seldom give more than a passing nod to the concept of an intellectual conscience. Nietzsche is one of the few who stress its importance. Now suppose we define a moral conscience as a kind of compass that orients us toward justice and that enables us to see that however pleasant, convenient, or tempting certain actions may be, they are nonetheless wrong, either because they do harm, or because they infringe upon someone's rights, or because they violate some other principle of behavior deemed to be of great importance. We might then define an intellectual conscience along parallel lines: it is a kind of compass that orients us toward truth and that allows us to distinguish between beliefs which enjoy some real probability from those which attract attention to themselves only by being pleasant, convenient, popular, spiritually gratifying, morally inspiring, or what have you. And just as a moral conscience pricks us when we flout justice in favor of passion or personal gain, so an intellectual conscience ought to sound the alarm when, in our thoughts or actions, we disrespect the value of truth.

Almost everyone—certain criminals and sociopaths excepted—possesses a moral conscience. The intellectual conscience is quite different, for the bulk of mankind either possesses no such thing, or they possess it only in the most rudimentary form. We are taught as children not to tell outright lies, but beyond that most of us know nothing of conscience when it comes to the conduct of our intellectual lives, and so we tend to let our minds do whatever they please. Nietzsche, though, is right: for anyone who fancies himself to be among the "tolerably free-minded people" of this world, an intellectual conscience is essential. To permit that conscience to sleep upon any excuse is shameful.

I have no desire to be an obnoxious atheist. I do not argue with the Jehovah's Witnesses who come knocking on my door. I do not tell people off when they wish me a merry Christmas. I do not even oppose the expression of religious beliefs in public life. If the students at some high school wish to form a prayer group, or a courthouse displays a copy of the Ten Commandments, that is no skin off my nose. The principle of the separation of church and state embedded in our Constitution does not, in my view, require public officials to feign agnosticism whenever they are on the job. Theists still constitute the majority of our citizenry; they have every right to live according to their lights, on weekdays as well as on Sunday, and on public property as well as on private. I must, however, make my reservations about their beliefs known, and this I do though my books. "God" and "faith" are the prettiest words in the English language—they have been lulling intellectual consciences to sleep for centuries. It would be shameful if I did not keep saying that.

Section 9

SNARLING

I first read William James's essay *The Will to Believe* over thirty years ago. I have reread it at least a dozen times since. James is one of my favorite authors not despite but because of his opposition to everything I believe about philosophy. His methods, attitudes, and conclusions all seem to me entirely wrong-headed. I am afraid I cannot recycle any of his bricks. He is still fun to read; his errors are both interesting and instructive. James has furthermore provided me with the raw material for my title, so I thank him for that.

Near the end of *The Will to Believe*, James accuses religious skeptics of churlishness. We wrap ourselves in a "snarling logicality," he says, by obstinately refusing to take anything on faith, when what we ought to do is approach the universe with "a more trusting spirit." The proper way to display a trusting spirit is to accept religious propositions without evidence. James even insists that when it comes to religion, belief might be a necessary precondition for the discovery of evidence. The gods will not make our acquaintance, he claims, unless we confer upon them in advance the favor of our credulity.

Over the last five thousand years, literally billions of people have performed the experiment in religious belief that James recommends. Have any of them discovered compelling evidence for the articles of their various faiths? Is there any reason to suppose that religious folk have made the gods' acquaintance anywhere except in their own imaginations? No, on both counts. You would think that if such reasons or evidence were ever to be forthcoming, then they would have come to light by now.

The idea that certain propositions must be believed before the evidence for them can be found is quite absurd. In fact, it is little more than an attempt to lull our intellectual consciences to sleep by making gullibility seem virtuous.

James provides a secular illustration of his meaning. Suppose a man to enter into a company of gentlemen previously unknown to him. Must he not accept their honesty on faith, before engaging in the kind of social interactions which would prove their honesty? Surely in this kind of situation trust comes first, evidence after. But I think James is mistaken, and that we can turn his own illustration against him. In order to socialize with our new friends, we need not accept the factual belief that they are all honest. We need only accept the moral belief that our peers deserve the benefit of the doubt until such time as their own behavior proves them to be scoundrels. Giving people the benefit of the doubt is a matter of action. In social situations we can act in a trusting manner toward our fellows, even though we may be agnostics regarding their personal merits. Factual beliefs concerning their honesty or reliability can always be held in abeyance until the results of our intercourse become known.

Agnosticism concerning any matter of fact need never compromise our ability either to act or to inquire. When we cannot act on the facts, because we do not know them, we are still free to act on what we take to be the ethical contours of our situation. And this, of course, is something we should do anyway, no matter what our epistemic predicament might be.

I am therefore happy to approach philosophical issues with a "snarling logicality," and to call myself not just a freethinker but a snarling logician. To be a snarling logician is to incorporate a measure of mistrust into one's method for doing philosophy; it is to embrace skepticism as an ongoing feature of one's philosophical constitution. A snarling logician directs his mistrust at philosophers who claim to have unraveled the cosmic play. He casts a skeptical eye on knowledge claims that seem to him poorly supported. He considers it part of his job to speak out whenever he catches the emperors of philosophy going about without clothes, or when they wear rags and call them three-piece suits.

Snarling is hard, on both oneself and others. There must therefore be an ethics to the practice of snarling. One should snarl with some degree of civility and good humor. One should snarl only at errors, fallacies, and muddled thinking, never at people. The authors one uses for diagrams should always be the best and brightest of thinkers, examples of great minds gone awry. It is important to remember that these authors are not just the agents of their errors but also their presumably unwitting victims. "Hate the sin; love the sinner," as Christians often say—and what goes for sins and sinners ought to apply with equal force to philosophical mistakes and mistaken philosophers.

This distinction between sin and sinner will be lost on some. People identify with their beliefs and with the methods used to arrive at them. They love their holes and will take it personally when the barricades surrounding those holes are attacked. Consequently, a snarling logician cannot avoid sometimes giving offense. It is the price paid for arguing honestly and with vigor on behalf of one's position.

My position, baldly put, possibly offensive, possibly even wrong, but articulated over the next two essays, is that there is no God and that faith is bad for the brain. In defense of this position, I will try to do what David Hume claimed to have done with regard to miracles. At the beginning of his discussion of miracles in *An Inquiry Concerning Human Understanding*, Hume states:

> I have discovered an argument ... which, if
> just, will, with the wise and learned, be an
> everlasting check to all kinds of superstitious
> delusion, and consequently will be useful as
> long as the world endures.[xii]

It seems like a vain ambition, but without such ambitions philosophy loses its meaning. What are we philosophers trying to do, if not discover arguments sufficiently sound to stand the test of time, arguments which will suffice to enlighten the more perceptive members of future generations? No philosophic argument can persuade all. No philosophic argument can establish anything with complete certainty, or remove all doubt or possibility of error. That does not make argument futile. There is still a crucial difference between good arguments and bad ones. To demolish a bad one, or to clearly state a better, is to make progress in philosophy. It is the only kind of progress of which philosophy is susceptible, and the only kind it needs.

Section 10

THE FUNHOUSE MIRROR

Imagine two little boys arguing. One of them exclaims, "You're a jerk!" Although the other boy cannot let the insult pass, he cannot think of anything original to say either, so he flings the same insult back: "You're a bigger jerk!"

In book 1, chapter 2 of *Mere Christianity*, C. S. Lewis refers to atheism as a "boy's philosophy." He considers watered-down versions of Christianity (those that leave out the devil) to be equally childish, but real Christianity, he says, is the "manliest creed on the market." Why the gratuitous put-downs? I am guessing, of course, but I suspect that Lewis was only trying to give as good as he got. Perhaps he had been reading atheistic authors who had opined to the effect that belief in deities represented an infantile phase of human history that, hopefully, mankind would someday outgrow. Perhaps Christians of "liberal" views had made some unflattering statements concerning belief in the devil. Such commonly heard remarks must have stuck in Lewis's craw until he could return them in kind.

A similarly unimaginative exchange will no doubt take place with regard to my statement that faith is bad for the brain. The whole contents of *The Snarling Logician* will get reduced to that slogan. My detractors will oh-so-cleverly throw the comment

Andrew Marker

back in my face and say that what is really bad for the brain is lack of faith.

Elsewhere in *Mere Christianity*, Lewis employs the argument from morality. He tries to infer the existence of God from the existence of moral values. Human cultures throughout history, says Lewis, have always distinguished right from wrong. Although different cultures draw the distinction differently, there are still significant cross-cultural similarities indicative of a single Moral Law believed in by all normal human beings. From the Moral Law it is just one step to a Law Giver, which is to say, God. I will gladly concede that there is a real difference between right and wrong, an intuitive awareness of which is embedded in our human nature. If Lewis wants to call whatever it is that we are aware of the Moral Law, I have no objection. I know of no better term for it. Yet even with this concession, Lewis's reasoning remains faulty. The Moral Law can only provide a very general guidance as to what ought to be the case on earth. It has absolutely nothing to say about what—if anything—is the case in heaven. One can imagine a legislator behind the law, just as one can imagine an angry Poseidon being responsible for some stormy seas; but there is no legitimate inference from one to the other.

In his essay on the theological virtue of hope in the same volume, Lewis argues for belief in immortality:

> The Christian says, "Creatures are not born with desires unless satisfaction for those desires exists. A baby feels hunger: well, there is such a thing as food. A duckling wants to swim: well, there is such a thing as water. Men feel sexual desire: well, there is such a thing as sex. If I find in myself a desire which no experience in this world can satisfy, the most probable explanation is that I was made for another world."[xiii]

What a bizarre line of reasoning Lewis offers us in this passage! He speaks as if nature provided for its creatures as generously as wealthy human parents do their children, lavishing its bounty on them so that want and frustration are virtually unknown. But nature is neither so benevolent nor so well endowed with the good things living beings desire. Yes, there is water in the world, but only in finite quantities. How many fish have died sucking at air because the stream they depended on had dried up, or their pond had evaporated, or because sea levels had fallen? Babies of many species feel hunger, but food too is a scarce resource, and so the offspring of countless mothers have died in uncomprehending misery during prolonged famines. Human beings desire life, love, and happiness. Those things are available, but again, only in finite quantities, intermittently doled out. If the inconstancy of our happiness, the imperfection of our loves, and the brevity of our lives frustrate us and leave us craving more, how exactly does that entitle any of us to live forever basking contentedly in the infinite love of an omnipotent super-being? How are examples drawn from nature supposed to authorize an inference from human yearnings to metaphysical realities? Pretending that such inferences are warranted is exactly the kind of wishful thinking that, in other contexts, Lewis claims to deplore.

Theistic arguments seldom get any closer to being cogent than do these two from Lewis. Theists offer bad arguments for their beliefs; when those are exposed as fallacious, they move on to others equally atrocious. When those too are exposed, theists begin to offer bad arguments for thinking that better arguments are unnecessary. Faith has a funhouse mirror effect on reason. It makes dreadful thinking appear sensible. This is why I maintain that faith is bad for the brain and why I prefer to stick with the religious skepticism I adopted as a boy.

THE FOLLY OF FAITH

Section 1

DIMENSIONS

Beliefs are cognitive dispositions. A belief is a way of seeing the world, remembering it, evaluating it, imagining its possibilities, or anticipating its future. Every belief relates to some proposition; this is why beliefs are often called propositional attitudes. To believe a proposition is to have some willingness, inclination, or tendency either to affirm that proposition in our thoughts or to express our allegiance to it through our actions. Once accepted into our network of beliefs, a proposition becomes both a lens through which we view things and the funnel that guides our responses to them.

Beliefs vary along three dimensions. The first is probability. We may judge a proposition impossible, unlikely, probable, or certain. In principle, we might assign a specific numeric probability to a belief: "I believe with .732 probability that I had eggs for breakfast last Tuesday." In practice, such evaluations are incredibly rare. Still, every belief is attended with some greater or lesser degree of confidence that is proportionate to the proposition's perceived probability.

The second dimension is hardness. One can imagine a Rockwell scale for beliefs. Rub two minerals together: the harder one stays intact, the softer one gets scratched. Similarly, when two of our beliefs conflict, one may survive at the expense of the other's rejection. By definition, the survivor enjoyed the greater hardness. Generally speaking, hardness will go along with probability. If our belief that *P* seems inconsistent with our belief that *Q*, the belief that seems the more probable to us will also be the one we are most likely to retain. There are exceptions to this rule. Consider this scenario: The propositions *P* and *Q* conflict; *P* appears more probable than *Q*; yet we resolve the tension by abandoning our belief that *P*. We continue to believe that *Q*. This will be quite rational if, of the two beliefs in question, the *Q*-belief is the more firmly embedded in our belief network. To abandon our belief that *Q* would thus require a thorough restructuring of our beliefs, and the abandonment of many thought to be well established. If our *P*-belief can be dropped with fewer and less severe consequences, then our natural conservatism will lead us to cease believing that *P*. We will conclude that *P*'s former appearance of enjoying greater probability was an illusion.

The final dimension is rank. Suppose we believe both *P* and *Q*, and there is no logical conflict between them. We may still need to choose, in a given situation, which belief we prefer to act on. If I am a juror at a murder trial, I may believe that the defendant is guilty and that his brutally slain victim deserves justice; yet I also believe that there is some doubt in the case, and that every defendant deserves the benefit of the doubt. Consequently I vote to acquit. Here one set of beliefs has been given priority over another. It has "pulled rank." I act on the higher-ranking beliefs while suppressing my desire to express the others.

Beliefs differ from methodological presumptions. While both can be described as propositional attitudes, the former carry genuine conviction, but the latter do not. Methodological presumptions mimic the behavioral effects of beliefs, yet lack the underlying cognitive foundations. The mimicry involves no intent to deceive; quite the contrary—the purpose of methodological presumptions is often to bring truths to light. Think again of the murder trial. The defense attorney does not necessarily believe that his client is innocent. He may have an opinion on that subject, or he may not. What he does believe is that his client is both legally and morally entitled to the best defense possible and that mounting such a defense requires the attorney to act as if his client was innocent. Innocence thereby becomes the attorney's methodological presumption. No legal case could proceed unless the participants were willing to adopt presumptions of this kind. Similar presumptions are essential in all professions involving inquiry. They also make their presence felt in many activities of daily life.

What does it mean to say that we are "acting on a belief," or acting "as if a belief was true?" A belief may prompt us to commit a heterogenous set of acts, the nature of which depends on many personal factors. Our other beliefs, our desires, and our character all have something to say in the matter. Imagine finding a wallet on the sidewalk and discovering hundreds of dollars inside. Your belief that the wallet holds a large sum of cash may prompt you to seek out the owner and return the money to him; it could also prompt you to pocket the cash, and then go on a spending spree. Which direction you take is a question of character, not of belief.

Section 2

ABSTRACTIONS

Imagine that we are watching a movie. The movie consists of discrete frames, each of which is basically a still photograph. Yet we never see any of those frames. All we ever see is a single continuously changing image on the screen. Even though we know the frames are there, the movie still fools our brains into interpreting what we see in terms of persisting objects that move through the imaginary space and time occupied by the movie's fictitious characters. The movie can accomplish this deception because the number of frames is very great, the difference between one frame and the next is very small, and the frames flit by far too rapidly for our brains to separate them.

Beliefs have to do with those abstract entities called propositions. It might therefore be supposed that beliefs too must be abstract entities and that consequently our minds are full of abstractions. But this does not have to be the case. It is far more likely that mental phenomena—beliefs, ideas, thoughts, and so on—are just higher-order features of the brain. The brain generates those phenomena by constituting what Aristotle would call their material cause. Now clearly there is nothing abstract about the brain. Everything inside our heads is concrete and particular. Open up a human skull, and one finds only matter. So if this view is correct, beliefs cannot be abstractions;

they can only be concrete particulars embedded in a material substratum consisting of neurons, synapses, and electro-chemical impulses. How then can brain activity tie itself to propositions, ideas, or other abstractions? It accomplishes the task in roughly the same way a movie does, through the generation of an illusion. The illusion can occur because the number of neurons in a human brain is very great, its computational powers can register differences that are very small, and the whole system works with incredible rapidity. This permits the human brain to represent, describe, and exploit abstractions, even if it cannot contain anything that is an abstraction. Just as a movie does not actually have to be a continuously changing picture—it just has to simulate continuity well enough to be indistinguishable from it—so too beliefs do not actually have to be abstractions; they only have to mimic abstract functionality well enough to create the appearance of a true (but physically impossible) abstraction.

Section 3

TABULA RASA

Think of a blank sheet of paper. We can write anything on it we want. We can use a typewriter, a laser printer, or scribble in crayon. We can use our own alphabet, Cyrillic letters, or Chinese characters. It does not matter. The sheet is equally receptive to any kind of writing, in any language, expressing any thought. John Locke portrayed the human mind as being rather like this. The mind, he said, begins its career empty, and gets filled with ideas as a result of experience. Locke used the word "idea" in many different senses, to cover all kinds of mental contents. According to at least some of those senses, he was probably correct: there are no innate ideas, only innate capacities to acquire them. Locke's imagery has the added virtue of celebrating the mind's tremendous potential. It does seem as though we are capable in principle of thinking an infinite variety of things in an infinite variety of ways, and thus of capturing the whole world in our thoughts, while making incredibly fine distinctions within it. Nor are our thoughts limited to the world, for we can conceive not only of what is, but of what could be, might be, or ought to be. In other respects, though, the image of the mind as a blank slate, or *tabula rasa*, seems fundamentally misguided. It attributes to the mind no structure, no preferences for learning one thing rather than another, and no ability to resist or filter the influences coming at it from the environment. Along with the potentiality of the *tabula rasa* comes a kind of passivity. One cannot help feeling that Locke's metaphor fails to capture something important about human nature. Perhaps a different image would help fill in the missing elements?

Section 4

THE MILL

Kant saw the problems in Locke's approach. He sought to fix them by initiating what he described as a Copernican revolution in epistemology. In the sixteenth century Copernicus turned astronomy on its head. Copernicus's predecessors had naively portrayed the sun and the planets as revolving around the earth, which is what they appear to an earth-bound observer to do. The most famous of these predecessors was the Greek astronomer Ptolemy, whose geocentric vision had stood with only minor modifications for well over a thousand years. Copernicus, however, postulated that the earth was just another planet. All the planets, he said, including the earth, revolved around the sun. This was a wildly counterintuitive notion, but it worked, and it eventually became the standard theory. Copernicus's insight represented a triumph of reason over naive common sense. Kant, writing in the eighteenth century, wanted to turn epistemology on its head in a similar fashion.

Kant's predecessors, most notably Locke, had taken the naive common sense view that reality imposes its order on us. The world has a spatiotemporal and causal structure that is quite independent of the human mind. When we perceive objects in the world, our minds register features of that structure. Kant, however, postulated that the world has no mind-independent structure, or at least none that we can discover. The world beyond our minds, considered as a collection of things-in-themselves existing apart from us, is a complete and impenetrable mystery. All we can ever know are how things appear to us. The appearances are the stuff of human experience; they are what we observe and what our scientific theories are about. Yet the appearances are just mental representations. They do not come to us ready-made. We have to construct them. The mind, given only the formless raw material of sensation, must impose on that chaos a spatiotemporal and causal order. The basic structure of the world of appearances—what Kant called the phenomenal world—is thus something of our own devising. That structure derives not from the world's intrinsic properties but from the innate ordering principles of the human mind. Epistemologically speaking, then, the mind does not revolve around the world; instead the world revolves around and depends upon the mind. At least this is true of the phenomenal world, the world as we know it. As for the transcendental world of things-in-themselves, Kant had to place that beyond the limits of scientific knowledge. It is a realm reserved for metaphysical speculation and religious faith.

Think of a steel mill. It uses recycled scrap metal to make giant tubes for oil and natural gas pipelines. Each day, trucks bring loads of junk to the mill: old washing machines, broken toasters, used cars, rusty railroad spikes, and so on. Furnaces inside the mill melt down all these items. The molten metal is purified of undesirable elements, creating new alloys that are then molded and pounded into pipes of various sizes and shapes. Trucks full of pipes can be leaving the mill from one end even as trucks containing junk are entering it on the other side. But suppose we could neither see the trucks entering the mill nor examine the junk inside them. Suppose we could only inspect the finished pipes. There would be no way for us to tell which pipes were made from toasters and which from automobile axles. We could not even tell if axles or toasters had been involved. For all we would know, the pipes might have been made from freshly mined ores. This is because the mill doesn't just use the junk; it destroys it. Nothing of the original character of the junk remains once it passes through the mill. The milling process obliterates virtually all of the information contained in that junk. We would thus have no means of inferring anything about the junk, based only on our observations of the pipes.

Although Kant does not employ this image of the mill, I think it accurately depicts his world view. Let the mill stand for the human mind. Let the realm of things-in-themselves be represented by the factories that make, and by the people who use and discard all those toasters, washing machines, automobiles, and railroad spikes. The trucks full of junk then represent the sensory impact that things-in-themselves have on the mind. The milling process is simply the mind's work as it constructs the phenomenal world of its experiences. The finished pipes are the phenomena themselves. Putting all those pipes together into pipelines that crisscross the country is a separate task, one that resembles not the mind's elementary work of experience construction but the more advanced work involved in our development of abstract philosophical and scientific theories.

Kant does succeed in highlighting the very features of the mind that Locke underestimated, namely that the human mind has a complex innate structure and that it is exceedingly active, even aggressive, in its cognitive intercourse with the world. Yet the Kantian cure might still be worse than the Lockean disease. In attempting to solve one problem, Kant created others even greater, problems that are probably insuperable within the limits created by his assumptions.

Kant thought he had discovered something important: his fellow human beings were thinking about minds all wrong. Being an unselfish philosopher, he wanted to share his wisdom with others. How did he plan to do that? For a metaphysical realist who believes that space and time exist independently of the human mind, explaining how one mind communicates its thoughts to others presents no great difficulty. One can express one's opinions by writing a book. Books, pens, and the light that reflects off a page and strikes the eye of a reader, these things exist apart from us and provide the physical medium through which ideas can pass from one mind to another, hopefully without too much distortion. But Kant was not a realist, so he could not account for human communication this way. In his view, books, pens, splotches of ink, and beams of light are nothing more than representations in the mind. They cannot leap from one mind to the next, nor can they supply us with any sort of medium between minds. How then did Kant account for human communication? The answer is: he didn't. His world view deprived him of the tools necessary to explain how people can share their thoughts.

I am pretty sure that I exist independently of Kant. I am not a mere phenomenon, or bundle of representations, in his mind. Relative to him, I am a thing-in-itself, and so belong to that permanently mysterious and unknowable realm beyond the confines of his mind. Likewise Kant, I presume, once existed as an independent Kant-in-himself, something quite distinct from the merely phenomenal Kant represented in my mind. Now Kant must have thought that it was possible for him, the real him, considered as a thing-in-itself, to communicate with me, not just the phenomenal me, but the real me. He wrote a book, *The Critique of Pure Reason*, in order to effect that communication, and in that book he explicitly declares his desire to bequeath the gift of his thoughts to future generations. But if what Kant says in that book is true, then his effort to make such a bequest must be futile. Kant, considered as a thing-in-itself, must be unknowable to me. My representations of him cannot provide me with any real information about him. If I accept Kant's philosophy, then I have no reason whatsoever to think that the views I attribute to the phenomenal Kant have any resemblance to the views that actually existed in his mind. All the information contained in

Kant's profound cogitations should have gotten obliterated during its transmission to me. Why, one wonders, should our knowledge of people be any better than our knowledge of other things-in-themselves, which Kant insists are unknowable? Nothing in Kant's philosophy allows us to distinguish the epistemic status of other people from that of rocks. In fact, given his outlook, we can't even be sure that there is any one-one correspondence between phenomenal objects and things-in-themselves. We cannot, for example, know that there is one and only one thing-in-itself corresponding to the phenomenal Kant, or even that the thing-in-itself that produces Kant phenomena for us is any different from the one that produces Hume phenomena, or Plato phenomena. So if Kant was right, and he did have some great insight, then he could not have told me or anyone else about it. If, on the other hand, he did tell the world what he thought about things, then the success of his communicative effort proves that he was wrong, and that his theory of mind must have been way off base.

Now consider the famous thought experiment in which we imagine ourselves to be bodiless brains stored in large vats. Let the vats be filled with some sort of solution that keeps our brains moist while providing all the essential nutrients: vitamins, minerals, sugar, and so forth. Our brains are connected by copper wires to computers built, programmed, and operated by a team of scientists. The computers send electrical signals through the wires, which cause us to have experiences. This creates the illusion that we have bodies, and that we can move around in space, interacting with other bodies and with people. We have no idea what is really going on. We know nothing of the scientists and their computers. Nothing in our experience corresponds to either the vats or the copper wires. In one version of this tale, the brains in the vats are entirely unconnected to one another. However, a second version allows the brains to interact. For example, when one brain thinks that it is talking, the computers send signals to nearby brains causing them to think that they are listening, and the words "spoken" will match those being "heard."

Call the scenario described in this thought experiment "Vat World." Odd though it may seem, Vat World is isomorphic with the world as portrayed in *The Critique of Pure Reason*. The two worlds have similar logical structures; they place us in basically the same epistemic predicament. Vat World merely gives concrete expression to things that Kant states abstractly. Kant's God is the homologue of Vat World's team of scientists. Kant's things-in-themselves are represented in Vat World by the network of vats, wires, and computers. Vat World takes Kant's minds and places them inside substances called "brains." Vat World thus models the world of Kant's Transcendental Idealism. It also suggests a solution to his difficulty regarding interpersonal communication. Kant could say that God has arranged things according to the second scenario. Somehow, through mechanisms wholly unknown to us, our thoughts get transmitted to our fellow human beings. Thanks to God's special dispensation, our experiences do contain accurate information about other people, and this constitutes a crucial exception to the rule that we have no knowledge of things-in-themselves.

Of course, we cannot know that God has made such a dispensation. We have absolutely no reason to suppose that anything of the sort has taken place. If we believe in this alleged dispensation, we must do so on faith. The same goes for belief in God. Kant rightly rejected all the traditional arguments for theism. But as I showed in my introduction, Kant's own reasons for accepting belief in God were no better than the ones he rejected. This leaves his theism with nothing to rest on except faith. Even the belief in a realm of things-in-themselves depends ultimately on a leap of faith, since there is no inference from the phenomena to things-in-themselves. All we can infer from the phenomena of nature are more natural phenomena, as Kant himself understood. All this talk of faith, though, merely covers up with a pretty word the ugly fact that our grounds for accepting Kant's world view are neither better nor worse than those for believing in vats, computers, and teams of mad scientists.

Philosophers engage in thought experiments such as Vat World because they provide us with tools for exploring certain logical possibilities. Vat World is such a logical possibility. Reality could be like that. Yet it would be crazy, literally crazy, to think that it actually is like that. Anyone who seriously believed themselves to be nothing more than a brain stored in a vat would have gone totally off the deep end. But if it would be irrational in the extreme to believe in Vat World, can it be any more rational to believe in its isomorph, the world of Kant's Transcendental Idealism?

A very basic logical principle is at stake here. If two arguments are isomorphic, differing only in their content, and one of those arguments is known to be invalid, then the other argument must also be invalid. Whatever fallacy infects the first must infect the second also, since fallacy and validity are the result of form, not content. Similarly, if two world views are isomorphic, and one of them is obviously crazy, then the second cannot be very rational either. Whatever defect makes the one crazy must also compromise the rationality of the other. We have already employed this principle in our analysis of Schopenhauer's philosophy. His theory of will might seem attractive at first, but its plausibility gets ruined when we realize that it is logically on all fours with an obviously ridiculous theory of gravity.

Now clearly Kant was not crazy. On the contrary, he was the Enlightenment's brightest bulb. Yet the same logical principle that brought Schopenhauer's metaphysic to ruin must also demolish Kant's. To understand the isomorphism between Transcendental Idealism and Vat World is to realize that Kant must have gone horribly astray in his reasoning. We need to correct his error, and this will involve changing our image of the human mind.

Section 5

THE VENDING MACHINE

The room where the reader is sitting right now probably has a smoke detector. Smoke detectors do something very simple: they detect smoke. When smoke is present, they sound an alarm. This can save people's lives. Hearing the alarm gives everyone within earshot an opportunity to flee the deadly fire that caused the smoke. Smoke detectors are thus also fire detectors.

One way to understand how a smoke detector works is to view it as an information transmitter. A smoke detector's environment contains information. Either smoke is in the room, or it isn't. The smoke detector has internal mechanisms that allow it to extract that information and convert it into action: it either sounds the alarm, or it doesn't. Sounding the alarm transmits information about smoke (and potentially also about fire) to those who may need it. Not sounding the alarm also transmits information. The smoke detector's silence assures people that they are not in any immediate danger.

The internal mechanisms involved in a smoke detector's operation represent not just order, but design. The manufacturer designed its smoke detectors to do this one task, and do it well. But to fulfill its purpose in a cost-efficient manner, a smoke detector has to have limits. For example, it may not be able to distinguish the relatively harmless smoke coming off a cigar from the much more dangerous smoke generated by a burning couch. And precisely because it is designed to be sensitive to smoke, a smoke detector will very likely be oblivious to other airborne gases, such as perfumes, skunk smells, or methane.

Although a vending machine is more complicated than a smoke detector, its purpose is essentially the same: to extract information from the environment and convert it into productive action. Here the information might be "Someone wants a Coke and has the money to pay for it." The action is then: "Dispense a can of Coke." A vending machine's mechanisms allow it to make much finer discriminations than a smoke detector does. A vending machine can tell the difference between a request for Coke, and one for diet Coke or orange juice. It can also distinguish between quarters and nickels, and between things that are US currency, and things that are not. There are still limits, though. The vending machine probably cannot tell Canadian from Mexican coins; it may be unable to accept Susan B. Anthony dollars. With vending machines, as with smoke detectors, engineering trade-offs are to be made between function and cost. The design that permits certain actions and discriminations also prohibits others.

These same principles apply to living creatures. Like a smoke detector or a vending machine, a frog's brain has internal mechanisms that capture information from its environment and then put it to work. For a frog, the relevant information might be "A flying insect is right in front of me." Upon receipt of this information, the frog's brain produces the appropriate response: "Snag insect with a flick of the tongue, and then eat." A frog's brain is far more complicated than any smoke detector or vending machine. Its mechanisms are more numerous, and the information it can handle is more diverse. Yet the frog's brain also has limits. It can tell flying insects from crawling ones but not male insects from female insects. Such limits are a matter of design. Evolution has designed the frog's brain to consider some bits of information more important than other bits. Evolution has to work within the same kind of engineering constraints and trade-offs that human manufacturers do. Investing a brain with a discriminatory power imposes a cost, a cost that must pay for itself through increased reproductive success. Frogs evolved the ability to tell flies from spiders because that ability aided their survival. Distinguishing male from female flies would be less helpful to them, so an ability to make that distinction would be less likely to evolve.

What goes for frog brains goes also for human brains, and hence for human minds. The human mind can very properly be seen as an extremely sophisticated network of mechanisms that have been built into our brains by the Darwinian process of evolution through natural selection. That process has designed our minds to extract information from the environment and convert it into adaptive behavior. I cannot say that this is all our minds do, for once our mental mechanisms evolved it became possible for us to put them to many uses unconnected to survival and reproduction. Yet the fundamental process of information extraction and conversion still stands at the core of what our minds do. Biologically speaking, it is what our minds are for. All of our methods of belief formation are just so many tools designed for the achievement of that purpose. Our beliefs are the natural by-product of this information processing system.

Our minds too have limits. For example, we can see objects only if they reflect light from a very narrow band within the electro-magnetic spectrum. To infrared and ultraviolet light we are oblivious. In fact, we are oblivious to most of the information in our environment. Some of the information out there seems relevant to us; the rest we ignore. We thus pick and choose what information to extract, and we sort through it using concepts and classificatory principles that are highly idiosyncratic. Other species, for example, might parse out the visible portion of the light spectrum using a color scheme entirely different from the one we employ.

What occupies human brains is not so much a network of mental mechanisms as a hierarchy of them. We have mechanisms for turning stimuli into behavior; we have mechanisms for turning other mechanisms on and off; we have mechanisms for modifying mechanisms. We could even have mechanisms for turning on the mechanisms that modify the timing on mechanisms that do reconstruction work on the mechanisms that directly control behavior. Such a hierarchical arrangement endows our minds with incredible flexibility. It makes it possible for us to learn a second language, change careers in middle age, and become converts to newly formed religions.

With flexibility comes freedom. We are not chained to our nature, because our nature is plastic, and because it allows us to respond intelligently to our environment; neither are we enslaved to our nurture, since we learn only what we want to learn during our upbringing, and this is sometimes very different from what others intended to teach us. What I have just described may not be the absolute metaphysical spontaneity philosophers and theologians dream of. It is not freedom from mechanical causation, but rather a freedom generated by such causation. Still, it is a freedom well worth having, and it replicates the functionality of metaphysical freedom so well that in most cases the two are virtually indistinguishable.

Kant was right: the human mind does possess innate structures that determine *a priori* how we are going to experience things. Our minds are not the passive recipients of impressions from outside, but active agents whose decisions and natural inclinations help to shape our cognitive intercourse with the world. In other respects, however, Kant blundered. He thought that by imposing the concepts of space and time on sensory stimuli we in effect destroy whatever information those stimuli contained. Since the order we impose has nothing to do with whatever order might be intrinsically present, experience leaves us devoid of any real knowledge of things as they are in themselves.

Yet the imposition of our conceptual structures upon stimuli does not destroy information—it captures it. The photons that hit our eyes, the sound waves impacting our ear drums, and the traces of chemicals filtering into our noses are chock full of information about the world around us. Although our strategies for capturing that information may be imperfect, idiosyncratic, and limited in scope, they do lead us to acquire genuine knowledge of how things are in the world. If knowledge of things-in-themselves really was impossible, as Kant supposed, then it would also be impossible for us to respond to those things in an intelligent manner. How would we ever know what to do, if we had no information upon which to base our decisions, and if all of our ordinary beliefs concerned a merely phenomenal world existing only in our own heads? Kant's intense concern for morality and for mankind's practical interests should have led him to realize that those interests could not be served unless the knowledge his philosophy denied us was possible after all.

Conduct the following thought experiment: what would happen if, per impossible, a human mind was suddenly plucked out of its body and thrust into a world whose logical structure bore no resemblance to the spatiotemporal structure we are accustomed to? The *tabula rasa* of a Lockean mind would passively receive impressions, acquire a whole suite of new ideas in the process, and quickly come to learn of the world's structure, all with no more difficulty than it encountered when first learning about objects in space and time. A Kantian mind, on the other hand, would never even know that anything had changed. It would receive stimuli from that brave new world, impose a spatiotemporal order on them, and go right on experiencing phenomena no different in kind from those it had encountered before. But if the view advocated here is correct, then something entirely different would occur. The mind presented with alien and unrecognizable stimuli would experience chaos. The subjective feeling might resemble that of listening to static on the radio or looking at snow on a television screen. If the mind could not create at least an approximate fit between concepts and stimuli, it would have to reject those stimuli, just as a vending machine designed for US currency rejects Mexican pesos, or gets jammed and malfunctions when loaded with laundry tokens.

So is the human mind just a glorified vending machine? Well, no, I am not saying that. What I am saying is that the vending machine image is a useful one. It retains the best features of Locke's *tabula rasa*. There is no reason why a mind built out of thousands or millions of bits of neural machinery should not simulate the receptivity of paper well enough in most situations to produce the illusion of being an excellent *tabula rasa*. The vending machine image also preserves what is right about the Kantian point of view. A vending machine represents order designed for a purpose; its form is married to its function; the price it pays for being extremely good at some things is that it must be extremely bad at doing countless other things. It has limits beyond which it cannot go. All of this is true of minds also, just as Kant insisted.

Section 6
THE BISHOP

Space and time, said Kant, are empirically real but transcendentally ideal. They are not "out there" in the world beyond our minds. They are only aspects of the reality we construct within our minds. That in a nutshell was his Copernican revolution. I believe that he was mistaken and that our ordinary common sense realism is closer to the truth than is his transcendental idealism.

Consider again the analogy between the human mind and a piece of machinery. Although a smoke detector has innate mechanisms that predetermine that it can detect smoke and only smoke, the fact that a smoke detector has gone off is still evidence that there is smoke in the room, real smoke that exists independently of the smoke detector's activities. A vending machine likewise has innate mechanisms that constrain its responses, yet if such a machine dispenses a Coke, that is usually proof of someone's being thirsty. It should be no different with us. We experience a world of objects interacting in space and time because our minds possess innate mechanisms for generating experiences of that sort. Given those mechanisms, we could not experience the world in any other way. Yet the fact that we experience a spatiotemporal world is evidence, even compelling evidence, that such a world really exists "out there." We do not "construct" it, any more than a smoke detector "constructs"

Andrew Marker

smoke, or a vending machine "constructs" either its customers or their coins. Instead we simply observe that world and detect the objects in it, in precisely the same sense that smoke detectors detect smoke, and frog brains detect the presence of flies.

How did Kant come to conclude otherwise? Why did he think that a revolution was required? To understand the origins of Kant's thinking we have to examine the writings of the Irish bishop George Berkeley. Berkeley advocated a form of idealism very different from Kant's. His philosophy consequently represented a half-way house along the path from Locke's realism to Kant's transcendentalism. In Berkeley we find the arguments and insights that laid the groundwork for the Kantian revolution.

Berkeley inherited from Locke the belief that we perceive nothing but our own ideas. Locke took this counterintuitive belief entirely for granted. He simply defined "ideas" as whatever the mind is attending to when it thinks about, perceives, or imagines anything. Berkeley, though, argued for this position at great length. His arguments focused on the relativity and subjectivity of all human perceptions. An oar looks straight while resting in a canoe; place the oar in the river, and it looks bent. We might be inclined to suppose that the oar is really straight, and only appears bent in the water. But examine the oar under a microscope: once again the straightness disappears, and what we see is the irregular jagged line of peaks and valleys that mark the grainy surface of the wood. With greater resolution, even the jagged line could vanish, leaving us with just a chaotic swirl of molecules. The straightness, then, and the crookedness, too, were mere appearances, existing only in the mind. Berkeley applies this reasoning to all the sensible properties of physical objects. Here is what he says about tastes and colors:

> That which at other times seems sweet, shall to a distempered palate appear bitter. And nothing can be plainer, than that divers persons

56

perceive different tastes in the same food, since that which one man delights in, another abhors. And how could this be, if the taste was something really inherent in the food?[xiv]

If colors were real properties or affections inherent in external bodies, they could admit of no alteration, without some change wrought in the very bodies themselves: but is it not evident from what has been said, that upon the use of microscopes, upon a change happening in the humors of the eye, or a variation of distance, without any manner of real alteration in the thing itself, the colours of any object are either changed, or totally disappear?[xv]

Berkeley concludes that what we call material bodies are nothing but collections of perceptions, which can exist only in a mind. The world thus consists entirely of minds and their contents. There is not in addition to that anything that corresponds to the realists' material world.

Locke would agree that secondary qualities such as taste and color exist nowhere but in the mind. The primary qualities, though—shape, extension, mass, duration in time—enjoy a dual existence. They exist both in the mind as things perceived, and also in the objects. The perceptual quality is, he would say, a copy or likeness of the real property possessed by the object. The one represents the other by resembling it, in something like the way a statue both resembles and represents the person who was the statue's model. Berkeley demolishes this position. He correctly insists that all the arguments he deployed with regard to secondary qualities apply with equal validity to the primary qualities. Space and time are just as relative to the observer as color and taste. A perception, furthermore, cannot resemble anything but another perception. As Locke admits, we never see, taste, or hear anything but our own perceptions. Even if physical objects existed, they would be entirely imperceptible. But how can anything invisible "look like" something that is visible? And how could something that by definition is inaudible "sound like" anything we can hear? Obviously matter cannot have any of the sensible properties we normally attribute to it. The natural inference would seem to be that matter, considered as a collection of things in themselves existing beyond our minds, must be unintelligible and unimaginable, a something that from our perspective is indistinguishable from nothing.

Where then do our perceptions of bodies come from, if not from a mind-independent material realm? They come from God, of course. We see houses and streets, and apples on apple trees, because God inserts ideas of those things into our minds. Although Berkeley suggests that perceptions involving other people might come directly from those individuals, he fails to explain how that would be possible. How could we insert ideas into other people's minds? Are we telepathic? It seems more likely that human interactions can occur only with God's assistance. In the absence of any physical medium, God himself has to be the spiritual medium through which such interactions take place.

God's involvement in perception makes God the immediate cause of every ill that befalls us. When a pedophile kidnaps, tortures, rapes, and finally kills some innocent little boy, God must help out by reading the pedophile's mind, and then producing the appropriate ideas of horror and agony in the child's mind. God is thus the active coconspirator in all our sins and crimes. After we die, though, it is only we who go to hell, while God gets off scot-free. Berkeley briefly considers this objection, only to dismiss it. He never seems to have grasped the absurdity and injustice of what his God was doing. To Berkeley a world free of matter, and ruled by an omnipotent spirit, seemed perfectly wholesome. He had, moreover, what he considered to be knock-down arguments proving that the world had to be as he described it. When it came to the problem of evil, Berkeley simply took it on trust that God knew what he was doing.

Berkeley is right when he claims that the perceptions in our minds cannot resemble any objects outside them. But in order to represent mind-independent objects, perceptions need not resemble them; they only need to contain information about them. My computer regularly beats me at chess. When we play, information about the game is stored inside the computer's memory. Yet nothing in the computer looks like a chess board. Open up the hard drive, and you will find nothing in there that is pawn-shaped or the least bit knight-like or rookish. The sequences of zeros and ones embedded in the hardware are just symbols written in an arbitrary computer language and bearing no similarity to anything beyond themselves. Yet those symbols contain all the information the computer requires to calculate the moves that checkmate me almost every time. Unlike the computer, I can actually see the board and the pieces on it. Yet my perceptions of the game are also symbols, symbols that are entirely arbitrary and relative to the peculiarities of human neural systems. So what? Those symbols lodged in my brain may not take on the shapes of kings or knights, but they still contain all the information I need to give the computer a tough match.

Berkeley points again and again to the notorious fact that the perception of an object will vary with changes in the observer, even if the object itself does not change. Any given object will look smaller if the observer stands farther away from it; it will look bigger if the observer sees it through a telescope. An equally obvious fact, which Berkeley consistently chooses to ignore, is that perceptions will also vary according to changes in the object, even if the observer and the other surrounding conditions remain fixed. Let a given observer view any object from a given distance and under a given light; the only way the object is going to appear bigger or smaller is if it really does either grow or shrink. Perceptions are thus relative to the object, as well as to the observer. This is the other side of the perceptual coin, and it is precisely this feature of perception that allows our admittedly subjective experiences to register objectively valid information regarding physical objects. Now if Berkeley was right to say that perceptible qualities must be in the mind, because they vary with changes in the observer, then it must be equally true to say that such qualities exist in the objects themselves, because they vary from object to object, and for the same object at different times, even when the observer remains unchanged.

According to the realist theory of perception defended here, perception is about information transfer rather than the sensuous content of experience. The subjectively experienced sensuous content generated in our brains is simply part of the vehicle by means of which the necessary information transfer takes place. We can therefore agree with Berkeley that the phenomenal redness of an apple exists nowhere but in the perceiving mind, while still insisting with Locke that there is also a property of redness existing in the apple, a property that consists of a power to reflect light in a given manner. As Berkeley noted, phenomenal redness and real physical redness are nothing alike; yet the subjective sensuous content that is in the mind can still give us objective information about the power that lies entirely outside and beyond it. That different perspectives on an object produce different subjective experiences of it is no objection to this version of realism. If we examine an oar when it is resting in the canoe, and again while it is in the water, and a third time under a microscope, all three views can deliver useful information to us. We certainly have no difficulty synthesizing these different perspectives into a single understanding of what the oar is like.

Suppose for the sake of argument that realism is true, and that material objects exist in space and time independently of any mental involvement. Would we not then expect perception to have the dual aspect already described, where one aspect concerns the relativity of perception to the perceiver, and another concerns its relativity to the object? And isn't that duality exactly what we find to be the case? But if realism predicts what actually occurs, then how can any of the facts to which Berkeley points serve as evidence against that theory?

Berkeley's arguments thus fail to establish any grounds for adopting either his or any other version of idealism. The refutation of those arguments removes the motive for Kant's "revolution."

Section 7

PERCEPTION

Do we perceive mind-independent material objects, as common sense suggests, or only our own ideas, as Locke, Berkeley, and Kant all agreed? Think once again of the smoke detector nearest you. It has no mind and consequently no ideas. It cannot detect smoke ideas because there are none for it to detect. It can only detect smoke, the real smoke, if any, in the room where it is placed. The earliest forms of animal life on earth were probably like this. Those primitive little critters must have had the sensory capacity to perceive objects in their environments. They could not have survived otherwise. Yet they had neither minds nor ideas. No phenomenology would have been attached to their perceptions. They would not have enjoyed any subjective experience of warmth or color. For them, perception would have been a purely mechanical information-gathering function of their nervous systems. Modern organisms such as bees, ants, and worms probably still operate in this mindless manner. They see and feel their way through the world without (in our sense) experiencing anything.

Now think of the frog and the fly. Does the frog perceive the fly or only fly ideas? Frogs are far more complicated than insects and worms, so it seems reasonable to think of them as having ideas in the very broad sense of that word employed by Locke and

Berkeley. But what good would it do the frog to perceive its own ideas? It cannot eat fly ideas, only flies. And to catch the fly and eat the fly, it must see the fly. Could the frog perceive fly ideas and then infer the presence of a fly? That seems obviously absurd. The making of inferences is an advanced intellectual operation, far too advanced for a little frog.

The frog, then, must see the fly. Does it also perceive fly ideas? I would say that it does not. Although the frog's head may be full of fly ideas, the frog perceives none of them, because it lacks the ability to become self-reflectively aware of its own internal mental states. Nothing in the frog's cognitive makeup permits it to engage in introspection. Although there is no doubt some sort of phenomenology attached to the frog's perceptions, the frog is blissfully unaware of that. Whatever phenomenology exists in the frog's brain must have evolved simply as an aid to vision; it is an extra piece of neural technology that augments the frog's powers of perception.

Humans are self-reflectively aware of their private mental states. We know a great deal about our ideas, and so may be said to perceive them. But we do not perceive only them. We also perceive objects in the external world. If frogs and ants can perceive physical objects, then so too can we. Would it not be ridiculous to deny to ourselves a basic cognitive power possessed even by ants? So we perceive both ideas and their objects, in slightly different but obviously related senses of "perceive." We perceive objects by acquiring ideas about them. The ideas are, as I have already said, part of the vehicle by means of which information concerning objects gets captured and processed in our brains.

Section 8

POWER

The great Stoic philosopher Epictetus began his brief classic *The Enchiridion* with these words:

> There are things which are within our power, and there are things which are beyond our power. Within our power are opinion, aim, desire, aversion, and, in one word, whatever affairs are our own. Beyond our power are body, property, reputation, office, and, in one word, whatever are not properly our own affairs.[xvi]

The captain of an aircraft carrier can neither turn his ship on a dime nor make it hover in midair, but he can chart his course and take refuge in what ports he pleases. The power we enjoy over our own opinions is similarly great, if not absolute. We cannot force ourselves to believe patent absurdities such as "Justice is blue" or "Three is half of twelve." We cannot turn beliefs on and off like a light switch—"I believe that Thomas Jefferson wrote the Declaration of Independence; now I don't; now I do again." Yet we can choose whether to inquire or not; we can approach subjects with either a skeptical or a credulous eye; we can conform our opinions to those of our parents and peers or rebel against them;

we can read only those authors we already agree with or immerse ourselves in the opposition's literature; we can train ourselves to scan our thoughts for signs of bias, spin-doctoring, and wishful thinking, or we can let our reflections flow along without such monitoring. We cannot change our minds about everything all at once, but over time we can reshape our opinions in accordance with whatever epistemic values and intellectual virtues we see fit to cherish. In short, we control what we believe indirectly by directly controlling how we think. Our opinions, then, are our own affairs, just as Epictetus claimed. We are responsible for them. And what we can control becomes subject to ethical considerations. There can thus be an ethics of belief.

Section 9

ATTITUDES

We are born knowing how to breathe. We learn to walk quickly enough without any instruction. But the separation of fact from fiction is an acquired skill, more like dancing the ballet than walking or breathing. When left to their own devices, our minds tend to develop all kinds of bad cognitive habits. We let our opinions drift along with the currents of our emotions. We rationalize when we should reason. We make excuses for the enchanting lies of which we have become the willing pawns. While no other animal on earth is as rational as we are, neither is any so eager to be irrational. Acquiring skill at truth discernment is thus not just a matter of developing a certain technical competence. Attitude matters. The soundness of our judgment depends as much as anything else upon the extent to which we value truth. What is it that reveals truths to us, by making one proposition appear legitimately more probable than another? In a word—*evidence*. Our respect for truth is therefore something we can only display by showing a proper concern for the evidential backing of actual or possible beliefs. The ethics of belief are to a large extent the ethics regarding our attitudes toward evidence.

Section 10

THE PREACHER

In 1877 W. K. Clifford, an English mathematician, wrote an essay entitled "The Ethics of Belief." When I read it twenty years ago I was enthralled; upon rereading it more recently, I was disappointed. Clifford wrote with the self-righteous tones of a minister, urging his congregation to avoid sin and temptation. To adopt even one irrational belief, Clifford believed, is a violation of one's sacred epistemic duty, a crime against humanity, and the first step toward barbarism. He therefore expressed his thesis in the most extreme terms possible:

> To sum up: it is wrong always, everywhere, and for everyone, to believe anything upon insufficient evidence.[xvii]

Clifford's thesis is known today as evidentialism. Although Clifford did not call it that, his bold assertion remains one of the best-known statements of the idea. This is unfortunate. Clifford may have done evidentialism more harm than good by casting it in so indefensible a form. Consider this counterexample: suppose that aliens have kidnapped you. They convince you that they will destroy the earth if you do not come to believe that *The Iliad* was written by Homer Simpson. "That is absurd!" you reply.

"I cannot bring myself to do it." "No problem," say the aliens. "We have a pill that will help you overcome your doubts. Take it, and the belief will follow." Would you take the pill? I hope so. Saving humanity is far more important than preserving your knowledge of ancient Greek poetry. Yet taking the pill violates Clifford's maxim.

Clifford was still basically on the right track. He merely overstated his case by trying to produce an absolute and dogmatic "Thou Shalt Not!" Perhaps we could reformulate his core notion in more circumspect terms, while at the same time revealing the ethical issue that that notion is meant to address:

> Modest Evidentialism: It is dishonest, and therefore generally wrong, to believe propositions that lack sufficient evidential support. Honesty requires that we grant to each proposition no more credence than the evidence available can justify.

Casting evidentialism in terms of honesty is totally in keeping with Clifford's outlook. Believing without evidence, Clifford said, is like stealing; those who flout evidentialism in any matter are trying to steal a piece of knowledge, instead of earning it through the hard work of evidence gathering and evidence assessment.

The idea of proportioning one's belief to the evidence goes back to John Locke, from whose *Essay Concerning Human Understanding* both Clifford and I have borrowed a brick. Locke clearly understood the ethical dimension of evidentialism. A willingness to proportion belief to evidence, he said, is the mark of a lover of truth. Anyone who believes beyond what the evidence warrants displays not a love of truth but the love of some particular opinion, be it true or not. Clinging to poorly grounded opinions is philodoxy, not philosophy. Locke also grasped the connection between evidentialism and religious faith. In a world containing many competing and conflicting faiths, how are we to tell which faith is the true one, or if any are true? Obviously one cannot appeal to faith here, since faith is precisely what is in question. One must exercise one's reason by considering the arguments offered on behalf of different faiths and by examining the evidence supporting each.

Although Locke expressed a more moderate version of evidentialism than did Clifford, his views have likewise come under much attack over the years. To the extent that Locke tied his evidentialism to a now obsolete theory of ideas, those attacks may have been at least partially justified. Consequently I will not attempt to defend either Locke's evidentialism or Clifford's, only my own. The core notion of evidentialism is sound. Even so, the devil is in the details. Get the details right, and evidentialism makes perfect sense; get them wrong, and one produces a muddle. A number of points need to be made in order to explain what exactly modest evidentialism entails.

Section 11

IMPERATIVES

The principle of modest evidentialism should be taken as a hypothetical, not categorical imperative. It applies only on the assumption that truth, knowledge, and intellectual integrity are our top priority. *If* we value those things, *then*, according to our principle, we ought to let the evidence, or the scarcity thereof, constrain our credulity. Now of course if anyone freely admits that they care not a fig for truth, then there is nothing we can say to them. Nor should we care what they say to us. They are not philosophers. But once someone claims to care about the truth of their beliefs, or to know what the truth about any important matter is, then they enter our domain, and our principle applies.

So interpreted, evidentialism cannot be refuted by counterexamples such as the one described above. Taking the aliens' pill was morally justified because, and only because, in that situation the truth of a given belief was rightly deemed to be irrelevant.

Section 12

HONESTY

Imagine going to the hospital to visit a terminally ill friend. A former New Yorker, he asks you if the Yankees won their playoff game earlier that day. You did not watch the game, nor have you heard the final score, but you tell him that the Yankees did win. Your friend dies with a smile on his face just moments later. Now suppose that, unbeknownst to you, the Yankees beat Tampa Bay 6–3. Although you said nothing false, you were still dishonest. You pretended to possess a knowledge you did not have. You sacrificed your concern for truth in order to buy someone dear to you a final moment of joy.

Next, imagine that we are playing a game in which you flip a coin, and I try to guess whether it will come up heads or tails. Perhaps we make the game more interesting by placing small bets on the outcomes. I am entitled to guess either heads or tails, just as I please, and to bet whatever sums I can afford to lose. But if I guess heads, and bet on heads, does this mean that I must also believe that the coin will come up heads? Of course not. I have no reason to think heads any more likely than tails. As a good evidentialist, I must remain agnostic as to which way any particular toss will go. This hardly prevents me from continuing with the game. I can play simply for the fun of it, without claiming to have any insight into the future. But suppose

71

that after putting my money on heads, I begin to believe that your coin will land heads-up. "It will be heads this time for sure," I tell myself. "I just know it!" Am I not engaging in self-deception? Of course I might turn out to be right; perhaps the coin really will turn up heads. Even so, I am pretending to a knowledge I do not have. For the sake of inducing pleasant hopes, I have tricked myself into confusing preferred with probable outcomes. This is clearly dishonest, for exactly the same reasons that your words to your dying friend were.

Beliefs do not always involve knowledge claims. I might, for example, believe that there is a vast fortune in gold stored at Fort Knox without thinking that I know such to be the case. After all, I have never seen the gold, and have never met anyone who has. The government could have emptied the vaults at the fort without troubling themselves to inform the general public. But every genuine belief involves a presumption that one possesses information about the world. Beliefs are, if not knowledge claims, at least information claims.

Guesses and bets make no such claims. To say that I am guessing about any matter, such as a coin toss, is actually to admit ignorance. If I knew what the coin was about to do, or had any reliable information concerning the event, I would not need to guess. A bettor, on the other hand, could think himself in possession of special insight. If I go to the track and place twenty dollars on Philosopher's Folly in the fifth race, I might do so with the genuine conviction that he will win. Perhaps I have observed the horse during his workouts, noted steady improvements in his strength, compared the times he posts in training with the known performances of all the other horses, and determined that he is definitely the fastest thoroughbred in the field. Yet such conviction is not essential to betting. I might believe merely that Philosopher's Folly has a slightly better chance of winning than the 20–1 odds against him would suggest, and that this gives my bet a favorable risk/reward ratio. I could also be agnostic about the race; perhaps I am betting on Philosopher's Folly because, being a philosopher myself, I like the name, or because the horse's owner was my roommate in college, and I want to give the guy some moral support.

Pascal argued in his famous *Pensees* that we should approach religious faith with the spirit of a gambler. The evidence, he says, is inconclusive, and so the truth of religion may seem no more probable than not. But even if it were quite improbable, we should have faith anyway, because we lose nothing if we are wrong, and if we are right, then we gain infinite rewards. With such a favorable risk/reward ration, it is rational to bet on faith.

This argument, known as Pascal's Wager, rests on a flawed analogy. Beliefs are simply not like bets. Beliefs and bets relate to information in contrary ways, and so must count as animals of very different logical species. To opt in favor of the belief that P is not to wager on P's truth; rather, it is to acknowledge the receipt or discovery of whatever information P contains.

Accepting Pascal's Wager requires self-deception. Assuming for the sake of argument that Pascal is right when he insists on the ambiguity of the evidence, the only logical inference would be that we poor humans have neither knowledge of, nor any real information concerning, matters of religious significance. Honesty would then demand our agnosticism. If we take a leap of faith beyond the evidence, by gambling on the truth of some particular religion, we necessarily make a false information claim. We claim, falsely, that we have information which in fact no human being possesses. The religion we have chosen might indeed prove to be the One True Faith; even so, we were only guessing when we adopted it, while pretending that our guess was something more than that.

Pascal seems to have understood the points just made. He knew perfectly well that a decision to accept his wager could not by itself produce the desired beliefs. Such a decision could only motivate one to act as if the beliefs were true. For example, one could start going to church, saying prayers, taking Communion, and so on. He saw, however, that in time the endless repetition of religious rituals would lull the intellectual conscience to sleep, quell doubts, and bring forth genuine belief. The propositions of faith, which before had seemed no more probable than not, would then appear very probable. Proposition preferences would, in short, have transformed themselves through the alchemy of faith into proposition probabilities.

In its own sick and twisted way, Pascal's Wager is indeed quite rational. It is, however, a rationality not aimed at truth. The bettor who follows Pascal's proposal aims not at truth, but at salvation and the rewards of heaven. If then, any person wishes to take Pascal's Wager, in order to curry favor from a God who values dishonesty and treats self-deception as a virtue, let them do so. The evidentialist may still insist that if one prizes intellectual integrity, then the sophistry of the wager makes it morally abhorrent.

Section 13
EVIDENCE

Modest evidentialism applies primarily to what David Hume called "matters of fact and real existence." It provides a criterion for making judgments concerning such questions as whether Austin is the capital of Texas, or whether Copernicus was born in Poland. If valid at all, the criterion obviously applies also to questions regarding religion (e.g., "Is there a God?" and "Did Jesus rise from the dead?") We can, if we like, extend evidentialism to our beliefs concerning mathematics, logic, and moral philosophy, but such extensions are controversial, and it is not necessary to accept them in order to be an evidentialist. There can be many varieties of evidentialism, some more restrictive in their application than others.

Philosophers sometimes talk as if the only thing that could provide evidence for a proposition would be another proposition. This departs greatly from ordinary usage, for we commonly talk about many things being evidence besides propositions. We say, for example, that DNA and fingerprints are evidence at a murder trial, meaning by this not propositions about DNA and fingerprints, but the physical entities themselves. Narrowing the concept of evidence the way some philosophers do is arbitrary and leads to paradoxical results. Evidentialism in any of its more defensible varieties requires that we interpret the concept of evidence much more broadly. As a first approximation, evidence is just anything that might be logically relevant to the determination of a proposition's truth-value. It is whatever we must weigh, consider, observe, experience, or examine in order to render a correct verdict regarding a given proposition. "Evidence" is defined by the role it plays in our cognitive lives; whatever does the job of evidence *is* evidence. This definition allows for the existence of many different types of evidence. It permits evidence to bear a variety of relationships to propositions of different types.

Evidence is, in part, relative to the observer. What counts as evidence depends upon time and place, the other evidence available, and the observer's background knowledge. An irregularity in the apparent motion of the planet Venus might have been taken by medieval astronomers as evidence for a previously undiscovered epicycle; today a similar irregularity might be seen as proof that Venus's orbit around the sun was being perturbed by the gravitational pull of another celestial body, such as a comet. Evidence, though, is not just whatever people think it is. There is a normative element to the concept. Evidence is what a rational and informed observer ought to accept as such.

Section 14

JUSTIFICATION

Clifford begins *The Ethics of Belief* by telling the story of a businessman who owns an antiquated passenger ship. The businessman suspects that the vessel may no longer be seaworthy, but instead of going to the expense of refurbishing it, he quells his doubts with pleasant thoughts and finally convinces himself that everything is probably fine. The ship sinks on its very next voyage, everyone on board drowns, and the businessman collects on the insurance. The disastrous results make the businessman's negligence painfully obvious. In today's world the families of the dead would sue him for every penny he had. Clifford makes the additional point that the businessman would have been equally guilty of negligence even if the ship had not sunk. Should the vessel have made it to port with passengers and crew still alive, that would not have reduced the businessman's fault, it would only have meant that his moral failing would go unnoticed.

I have no quarrel with Clifford's conclusion. The businessman clearly engaged in self-deception regarding his ship's condition, and the dishonesty involved remains exactly the same, whether the ship makes it to port or not. This parallels the point I was making earlier about the terminally ill friend. Whether the Yankees won or lost, it was still dishonest to tell your friend that they won. Telling the truth can be dishonest if one tells it by accident; by the same token, believing a truth can also be dishonest, if one believes it by accident.

However, the parable of the shipowner seems to me to gloss over an important distinction, namely, the distinction between the justification of a belief and the justification of a believer. According to evidentialism, a belief is justified if and only if it enjoys adequate evidential support. A believer, on the other hand, may be justified if he remains honest in his judgments, performs due diligence in the gathering of evidence, assesses the evidence fairly, and makes a reasonable effort to arrive at the truth. A believer might do all that and still end up believing some poorly supported proposition. Should that occur, then the believer will be justified, even though his belief is not.

In Clifford's story, the shipowner and his belief about his ship were both unjustified. The belief was unjustified because there was no good reason to think that the creaky old vessel was still fit to sail. The ship's owner was unjustified because he failed to perform due diligence. He could have had the ship checked out and repaired, but he did not. The story might thus induce some readers to assume that an unjustified belief entails an unjustified believer, while a justified belief guarantees the justification of anyone who holds that belief. But that would not be a valid inference from the story. Personal failings such as dishonesty, prejudice, and negligence are not the only reasons why someone might adopt an improperly substantiated belief. Sometimes even the most rational people just make honest mistakes. Evidentialism need not be interpreted as offering any condemnation of them.

Section 15

REFUTATIONS

When properly understood, the principle of modest evidentialism articulated in section 10 becomes self-evident, even tautological. It basically asserts that when judging a proposition to be either true or false, we ought to give due weight to all of the available and logically relevant information, and only to that. Well, what else would we do? Ignore what we know? Consider data that isn't available? Emphasize factors that, by our own admission, aren't even relevant to the question at hand? How absurd!

There is something comical about efforts to refute evidentialism. The refutation can only consist of some argument that presents reasons for supposing evidentialism to be false. The anti-evidentialist fully expects that his audience will give all due consideration to the evidence he provides against evidentialism, and he hopes that they will proportion their belief or disbelief to that evidence. The refutation of evidentialism thus takes evidentialism entirely for granted, and cannot proceed without at least tacitly making evidentialist presumptions. This completely undermines the antievidentialist's case.

It would appear that while one can criticize specific versions of evidentialism, its core notion is hardwired into our brains. We can flout evidentialism in specific instances, either unwittingly or on purpose; but even the least rational among us instinctively follows evidentialist principles most of the time, and this is something we all must do, if our cognitive lives are to have any coherence.

"But flouting it only in specific instances, such as those touching upon religion, is precisely what I advocate," a fideist might say. "Can't we do that without abandoning reason altogether, or diminishing the coherence of our cognitive lives?" Is this not special pleading? And why should religion be granted this unique exemption from our ordinary standards of rationality?

Section 16

THE APPRAISER

Imagine that you are in the market to buy a home. With regard to each house you look at, you consider a number of things: its age and square footage; the number of bedrooms; proximity to schools, churches, and major highways; neighborhood crime rates; and the degree to which nearby houses appear to be well maintained. These are objective factors that any sensible homebuyer would care about, in part because they affect the price and potential resale value of each property. Based on such factors, there might be several houses on the market that would make perfectly appropriate homes for you, while still falling within your budget. How do you decide between them? This is where subjective elements come into play. Perhaps you decide to buy house A instead of houses B, C, or D because A puts you closer to your parents, or because you can hang your hammock between two trees in the backyard, or because you like the way the architect incorporated brick into the structure.

Mixing personal and impersonal factors in this way makes sense when buying a home or a car, or whenever we make practical decisions in life. To focus solely on the objective elements, while ignoring our feelings and visceral responses to things, would be foolish. In our practical reasoning we aim at happiness, our own and that of the people we love. To accomplish this we must listen

81

not just to our heads, but to our hearts. As Pascal put it, "The heart has its reasons which the reason does not know." With regard to practical decision making, he was right.

Now imagine that you are a property appraiser. It is your job to examine houses and provide an estimate of what each one is worth. With regard to any given house you might examine, the question you need to answer is not a practical one concerning whether you should buy it, but a theoretical one regarding the home's current market value. Assessing that value fairly requires you to put your personal feelings aside. Since you are not going to either purchase or live in the home, its suitability to your individual needs becomes irrelevant. What you need to focus on instead are the home's objective features, together with such things as the history of previous transactions, and the present state of the economy. If you overvalue a brick house because you have a fondness for brick, this would not exemplify listening to your heart; it would be a sign of incompetence. As a professional appraiser, you get paid not to listen to your heart.

Ask ten appraisers to estimate the value of some house— if they all do their jobs correctly, they should arrive at nearly identical results. The spread between the highest and lowest estimates should not be more than a few thousand dollars. Appraising a house involves skill; some of the appraisers might be better at their jobs than others. The extent of any appraiser's skill can be objectively tested by comparing her appraisals with the actual transactions on the houses she appraises. Buying a house is more art than science. Ask ten home buyers which house on the market they prefer, and they will give you ten different answers. No answer is right, and none is necessarily wrong; but if each of the ten gets a house they can enjoy for years to come, then in a sense all of them were right.

The distinction between practical reason and theoretical reason should now be clear. When we engage in practical reasoning, our passions can and should influence both the questions we ask (e.g., "What house should I buy?") and the answers we give (e.g., "I want that house!"). In theoretical reasoning, however, our passions should dictate only the questions we ask, never the answers we give. A property appraiser would not be working on houses at all unless some passion moved him to do so. He asks, "What is such and such a house worth?" only because someone is paying him to answer that question. The passion motivating his labors is thus the desire for money. Yet that same desire should not predetermine the results of his investigations. If an appraiser takes bribes to fudge his results, or if he inflates his estimates on certain properties to please his employer (perhaps in hopes of getting a raise or a promotion), then he is corrupt.

The basis for this distinction should be obvious: practical reasoning aims at happiness, which means different things to different people. Theoretical reasoning aims at truth, which is the same for all.

Section 17

THEORETICAL REASON

William James took a dim view of Pascal's Wager. In *The Will to Believe*, he critiqued Pascal as follows:

> We feel that a faith in masses and holy water, adopted willfully after such a mechanical calculation would lack the inner soul of faith's reality; and if we were ourselves in the place of the Deity, we should probably take particular pleasure in cutting off believers of this pattern from their infinite reward.[xviii]

James is being grossly unfair. Couldn't a faith that begins with a "mechanical calculation" eventually lead to faith of a more robust variety? I see no reason why it could not. Pascal was probably counting on it. It seems cruel of James's God to banish souls from heaven merely because they did some math. But James obviously had no use for the math. Passion, he thought, not mechanical calculation, is what ought to lead us into faith:

> The thesis I defend is, briefly stated, this: Our passional nature not only lawfully may, but must, decide an option between propositions,

whenever it is a genuine option that cannot by
its nature be decided on intellectual grounds;
for to say, under such circumstances, "Do not
decide, but leave the question open," is itself
a passional decision—just like deciding yes
or no—and is attended with the same risk of
losing the truth.[xix]

Deciding to adopt one religion rather than another, or deciding
between some religion and no religion, seems, on James's view,
to be a lot like buying a house. We can, and necessarily do, allow
personal concerns to supplement objective judgments. After all
the reasoning has been done, we let our hearts make the final call.
This sounds reasonable. At least James does not initially appear
to be engaged in special pleading, or asking that faith be given
some unique dispensation. Quite the contrary—he thinks the
decision-making model we ought to employ in religion should be
the exact same one we use in daily life, as when we buy a car or a
house, or decide whom to marry, or what city to live in.

Richard Kirkham, whose *Theories of Truth* is a landmark
study in its field, wrote this marvelously insightful passage about
James's mental habits:

The first thing we can say about William James
is that between his novelist brother Henry and
himself William has the clearer prose. The
second thing is that the first thing is not saying
much; clarity and consistency were not James
family traits. Part of the problem is that James
philosophically grew up in the later nineteenth
century, an era in which ambiguity, indirection,
and rococo encrustations of metaphor were
standard features of philosophical expression.
Also, if a characteristic feature of much

twentieth-century Anglo-American philosophy is the making of distinctions between things the ordinary man identifies, an equally common theme of the prior era was the conflation of things the ordinary man thinks distinct, the True and the Real being notable examples. Argumentation that preceding and succeeding generations would count as textbook indulgence in the fallacy of equivocation was elevated to a philosophic method in the world of James's intellectual upbringing. James's views never recovered from this intense early irradiation of nonsense.[xx]

In the passage quoted above, James is guilty of doing exactly what Kirkham accuses him of: he blurs together things that ought to be kept separate. Specifically, he tries to conflate the methods appropriate to theoretical reasoning with those that belong to practical reasoning. Deciding whether to believe or disbelieve a particular religious proposition is not like buying or declining to buy a house; it is more like appraising a house. Beliefs and disbeliefs are basically appraisals of a proposition's truth-value. Religious propositions do have objective truth-values, and this thrusts all questions about them into the province of theoretical reason. Here appeals to the believer's "passional nature" have no place. Our human passions can and should drive us to ask religious questions; they should not be dictating our answers.

James claims that our passions not only may, but must, dictate our answers. Suppose for the sake of argument that a certain question of great religious import "cannot by its nature be decided on intellectual grounds." Is it then really a "passional decision" if we opt for agnosticism? James answers in the affirmative. He would portray agnosticism on such issues as timidity: the agnostic timidly refrains from judgment for fear of being wrong. James advocates a bolder approach, one in which believers go with their hearts without fear of eventual contradiction. "Our errors are not such solemn things," he declares, and so aggressive risk taking is warranted.

James's manner of describing beliefs as if they involved risk shows that while he may have rejected Pascal's Wager, he still tacitly accepted its gambling metaphor. Like Pascal, he sees beliefs as being analogous to bets, and his position amounts to a call for bold betting. James ends *The Will to Believe* by quoting Fitz-James Stephen:

> We stand on a mountain pass in the midst of whirling snow and blinding mist, through which we get glimpses now and then of paths which may be deceptive. If we take the wrong road we shall be dashed to pieces. We do not certainly know whether there is any right one. What must we do? "Be strong and of good courage." Act for the best, hope for the best, and take what comes … If death ends all, we cannot meet death better.[xxi]

The mountain pass represents mankind's epistemic predicament, the blinding snowstorm our lack of insight regarding religious issues such as the existence of God or the immortality of the soul. This lack of insight should not trouble us, James is saying. Given such uncertain conditions, we should still be willing to make some bold conjecture as to which faith is correct, bet the fate of our souls on that guess, and so come to believe in the veracity of our chosen faith. This, James insists, is the courageous thing to do. The courage shown by the person of faith resembles the courage shown by mountaineers who navigate their way through a storm.

Is not what James is advocating in all essentials just what Pascal had also advocated? All James has done is change the imagery. Where Pascal put us at a race track, or on the casino floor, James puts us in the mountains, with the snow and wind whipping us in the face. James's imagery may be more dramatic, but the underlying logic is very much the same.

Were we travelers in the mountains beset by some terrible storm, we would indeed be forced to choose what path to take. Even if we did not know which path was the right one, still we would need to choose a path and make the best of it, since to do nothing, or to delay our decision pending the acquisition of further evidence, would mean certain death. But in this scenario, are we not just guessing which path is correct? And if we let some psychological alchemy transform our guess into a firm conviction, are we not engaged in self-deception? The philosopher in us ought to rebel against such deceit. Nor is there any reason why we could not act decisively, by picking and following some particular path, while still remaining agnostics about whether we have successfully chosen the right path. To hold fast to our agnosticism even under the stresses created by the storm would hardly indicate timidity; on the contrary, it would take considerable epistemic courage to withhold belief, when a claim to certainty would provide so much more comfort. Passing up such comfort would, furthermore, be prudent, for our agnosticism would keep us open-minded, and so make it easier for us to recognize our mistake, in the event that we take a wrong turn.

This reanalysis of the mountain pass parable emphasizes the crucial difference between action and belief. Actions *are* like bets. Bets are a species of action, and so make a good model for action in general. It makes perfect sense to speak of both actions and bets using the same language. For example, actions, like bets, may be described as either bold or timid. But beliefs are not like bets. When selecting one belief over another, we are not so much bettors as odds-makers. We are establishing the probabilities upon which bets and other actions might be based. Once this is understood, it will make little sense to speak of beliefs as being either bold or timid. To adopt an agnostic stance regarding any issue, whether religious or secular, is not to exemplify timidity, but rather to make an honest confession of ignorance. Similarly, to believe firmly in the truth of any proposition when evidence for it is lacking is never bold; it is self-deception and philodoxy, pure and simple.

We should not worry that our agnosticism on some issue of religious significance is going to lead to spiritual disaster. Our souls will not be "dashed to pieces," as Fitz-James Stephen put it. Here we can turn William James's own words against him, and insist that if agnosticism or disbelief be an error, then surely "our errors are not such solemn things." No God worth believing in would punish unbelievers either for their honesty or for their fidelity to the promptings of their intellectual conscience.

The distinction between theoretical and practical reason may be unfamiliar to Kirkham's "ordinary man." It is not, however, something concocted by twentieth century analytic philosophers. On the contrary, the distinction goes back to Aristotle, with whose *Nichomachean Ethics* James must have been acquainted. James would, furthermore, agree with me that on some theoretical issues our passional nature ought to be kept in check. Consider this passage from *The Sentiment of Rationality*, published about fifteen years prior to *The Will to Believe*:

> The future movements of the stars or the facts of past history are determined now once for all, whether I like them or not. They are given irrespective of my wishes, and in all that concerns truths like these subjective preference should have no part; it can only obscure the judgment.[xxii]

James is absolutely right. "Subjective preference" does "obscure the judgment" on all issues where truth or falsity rests not upon our wishes. I must thank James for so succinctly summarizing one of the central theses of *The Snarling Logician*. Why then does James back away from this thesis when religion comes into play? Is not the existence or nonexistence of God "given, irrespective of my wishes?" Is not Jesus's performance of miracles, or his rise from the dead, as determinate as any question about the stars' future movements? If so, then the truth claims of religion are not all that different from those made in science and history. Passions which cloud the mind on the latter issues cannot without special pleading be converted into oracles with regard to the former. If evidentialism applies to history and science, then it must apply with equal force to religion.

THE PARTY

I once received as a gift a copy of *Christianity: The Faith That Makes Sense* published in 1992 by Dennis McCallum. The parable in the first chapter, entitled "The Worst Party Ever," is hauntingly brilliant:

> Imagine yourself being ushered into a large party room with numerous booths, each offering a different activity or product. You can do anything you want at this party. There are thousands of people busily moving from one booth to another engaging in various pursuits. Some booths are offering art and music lessons. One popular booth offers assorted sexual experiences. Another booth offers drug experiences. A very large booth offers exercises which, when completed, will enhance one's body. Another offers tasks that entitle the participants to be rich. Yet another booth is a laboratory for scientific research.
>
> However, there is a problem. You can only stay at the party for a short time because, unfortunately, you have already been infected

with a virus that will kill you in three hours, if not sooner. The same is true for everyone else at the party. Everyone will die within three hours of the time they entered the party.[xxiii]

Life, says McCallum, is exactly like this awful party. It makes no essential difference whether our "party" lasts a few hours or several decades. Death "renders everything we do unimportant and meaningless in the end." What should we do? McCallum continues:

Back at the party, as you are wandering from booth to booth, you hear someone trying to get your attention. Looking over, you see a man standing by the corner of a booth near the wall, gesturing for you to come over. You walk over and ask him what he wants. He says "We've found a door here that the others don't even know about! You can walk out of this door and receive a cure for the virus that will enable you to live forever! You can return to the party and enjoy it …

Obviously, such a claim would make you suspicious. It might be a trick.[xxiv]

McCallum spends the remainder of his book arguing that it is not a trick. God exists; he loves us enough to provide us with the door we so desperately need. The "door" is, of course, Jesus Christ, who declares in John 10:9, "I am the door; if anyone enters through me, he shall be saved." McCallum does not ask us to take Jesus's promise on faith. He wants us to go by the evidence. *Christianity: The Faith That Makes Sense* is all about what McCallum takes to be "solid evidence" for his Christian beliefs.

I will not address McCallum's alleged "evidence." His arguments are not original; much of his discourse has to do with biblical prophecies, the untangling of which lies far beyond the scope of this book. My opinions concerning arguments both for and against God will be expressed in the next essay, and were also elaborated upon in *The Ladder*. What interests me about McCallum's work is the frame of mind with which he begins his inquiry.

That frame of mind seems guaranteed to create "subjective preferences" that "can only obscure the judgment." McCallum tells us that if we believe in God, and in his Son Jesus, then we can be happy forever; but if we do not believe, then we must spend our brief lives at a wretched "party" where death destroys all meaning, and fear of death destroys all happiness. Then he announces that we should decide between belief and skepticism *based on the evidence*!

The task that McCallum sets for himself and his readers is nearly impossible. No human being thrust into the predicament McCallum describes is going to be able to weigh the evidence in a rational manner. When we are desperate to believe, many bogus reasons for belief will seem like wisdom. Fallacious arguments that tell us what we want to hear will come to appear cogent. If our intellects force us to reject one argument, we will go to another, and then another, until our intellects are beaten into submission by our overwhelming desire to be happy. In short, we will accept whatever sophistries appear necessary so that we might escape our existential nightmare.

Imagine what would happen if the members of a jury were told, at the start of a trial, that if they vote for acquittal they will all receive big checks in the mail, but if they convict, they will be tortured for several days and then executed. Yet the jury is also told, by the same authority, that they should rule in favor of the defendant only if the evidence warrants. Could we really expect the jury to show the evidence much respect? A jury tampered with in this fashion would be corrupt from the start. No decision it rendered could be trusted. Clearly, though, if we accept McCallum's outlook, we become just like that corrupted jury. Our affections will have been tampered with so thoroughly that we will be unable to think straight.

McCallum has gotten things profoundly wrong. There may or may not be a God; Jesus may or may not be his Son; the human soul might be immortal—but perhaps it dies with the body. For each of these issues there is some objective truth to be discovered. We want to know the truth, so we inquire. But it is a grave error to insist that the results of our inquiry make us happy. Inquiry can do no more than modify our beliefs. And what are beliefs? They are propositional attitudes. The only relevant question regarding any belief is this one: Is the belief true? If it is true, then we can learn to embrace this truth and make it our own. We may even come to love the truth, however unpleasant it may at first have seemed. If, on the other hand, the original proposition turns out to be false, then its contradictory becomes our truth; we can embrace and love that. We need not fear that any truth will make us miserable. Happiness and misery emerge not from our attitudes toward propositions but from our attitudes toward life. Beliefs aim at facts. Life is about valuing those facts—putting the right "spin" on them, if you will. Our attitudes toward propositions, and our attitudes toward life, are logically independent. No matter what the facts of the world might be, no matter what our philosophical inquiries tell us is really out there, we are still free to adopt a positive, even spiritual attitude toward life. A world without God, without Jesus, and without immortality is only hell if we call it that and make it one. It is our choice. Some things, as Epictetus noted, are within our power—others are beyond it. Attitudes are within our power.

Must death, then, render "everything we do unimportant and meaningless in the end," as McCallum says? No, not at all—we might prefer to say instead that life no more loses its value by being brief than gold does by being rare. We might decide to value life, not because it provides a bridge to a better place (it probably doesn't), or because it is pleasant (more often than not it isn't), but simply because it is life.

Schopenhauer would have considered such talk to be quite silly. This is what he had to say on the matter:

> I cannot here withhold the statement that *optimism*, where it is not merely the thoughtless talk of those who harbor nothing but words under their shallow foreheads, seems to me to be not merely an absurd, but also a really *wicked*, way of thinking, a bitter mockery of the unspeakable sufferings of mankind.[xxv]

Schopenhauer, an atheist, chose to become a pessimist as well. He was free to do so. My only point is that we are equally free to do the opposite, by finding wisdom in what Schopenhauer called wickedness.

Section 19

FEAR

Let us turn our attention back to William James, who thought he had an answer to my earlier criticism that he had confused theoretical with practical reason. In a footnote to *The Will to Believe*, James explains how religious beliefs differ from ordinary historical or scientific beliefs, and why this justifies treating them differently:

> Since belief is measured by action, he who forbids us to believe religion to be true, necessarily also forbids us to act as we should if we did believe it to be true. The whole defense of religious faith hinges upon action. If the action required or inspired by the religious hypothesis is in no way different from that dictated by the naturalistic hypothesis, then religious faith is a pure superfluity, better pruned away, and controversy about its legitimacy is a piece of idle trifling, unworthy of serious minds. I myself believe, of course, that the religious hypothesis gives to the world an expression which specifically determines our reactions, and makes them in a large part unlike what

they might be on a purely naturalistic scheme
of belief.[xxvi]

For James, the decision to adopt a religious faith *is* a practical
decision, because by adopting a faith, one also commits oneself
to the way of life which that faith represents. Such an ethical
commitment necessarily involves our passional nature—the
heart, in other words, not just the head. Straightforwardly factual
beliefs of an historical or scientific nature do not typically involve
these ethical commitments, and so can safely be left to theoretical
reason and the intellect.

McCallum feared that if he did not accept what James
called "the religious hypothesis," then he could not be happy. At
bottom, James's thinking is also driven by fear—the fear that lack
of faith would diminish the ethical dimension of life. He seems
convinced that left to its own devices, theoretical reason would
lead us to the "naturalistic hypothesis," or what for practical
purposes amounts to almost the same thing, agnosticism. In
James's view, this would constitute a moral disaster, because said
naturalistic hypothesis can neither require nor inspire the right
actions. To reason only theoretically about religious questions is
thus to risk being diminished as people.

James has left himself no room for retreat; the quoted passage
forms the very bedrock of his position. Yet he is mistaken. Beliefs
are measured not by action but by truth. We are not entitled to
assume either that true beliefs must be morally inspiring or that
morally inspiring beliefs must be true. To make either assumption
is to lull our intellectual consciences to sleep with a noble lie, and
a noble lie is still a lie. If we cannot discover the truth through
rational investigation, then the only ethical response—because it
is the only honest response—is to confess ignorance and become
agnostic. We need not fear that agnosticism or even atheism
will lead to moral depravity. Whether we live moral lives or not
remains our choice. It is a question of character rather than faith.

Atheism certainly provides no excuse for immorality. Even we lowly atheists know right from wrong. If we fail to do what is right, then it is we, not our beliefs, that have failed, and so we have no one to blame but ourselves.

The religious and naturalistic hypotheses to which James refers actually differ very little when it comes to ethics. Murder, rape, theft, and arson are wrong, no matter what. Compassion, self-control, and common human decency are all virtues on either hypothesis. The love we bear toward our parents, siblings, and children, the affection we have for our friends, and the duties we owe to our countries, these things have nothing whatsoever to do with our metaphysics. To the extent that naturalism and theism do produce different ethical outlooks, we cannot determine which is better without first deciding which is true. So in the end it always comes back to the question of truth.

Hume had the key insight. He correctly argued that "is" does not imply "ought." We cannot infer how the world ought to be from the way it is, nor how it is, from the way we think it ought to be. This liberates ethics from both metaphysics and the natural sciences. It also means that, contrary to what James tells us, our reactions to the world cannot literally be determined by either the religious or naturalistic hypotheses. People are free to respond nobly to life whichever hypothesis they accept. They are also free to respond ignobly. The choice is within our power, and that is why we have nothing to fear from the ravages of theoretical reason.

Section 20

AUSTRALIA

Most objections to evidentialism stem from the two fears discussed: the fear of misery and the fear of moral bankruptcy. "The greatest terror," wrote Rabbi David Wolpe in his 2008 book *Why Faith Matters*, "is if the universe presents a blank face." The blank face of a universe devoid of religious significance or divine support seems to some intolerable; this leads them to seek spiritual certainties that evidentialism cannot supply. However, not all objections to evidentialism are so motivated. Some have a more technical nature. To address those, we will have to delve more deeply into how the concept of evidence functions.[xxvii]

Consider the forty-seventh proposition in book 1 of Euclid's *Elements*. It is one of the most famous passages in all of mathematics. Everyone who took geometry in school probably learnt this proposition or its equivalent. Proposition I.47 states that in any right triangle the square on the hypotenuse will be equal to the sum of the squares on the other two sides. What is the evidence for Proposition I.47? In section 13, I defined "evidence" as "anything that might be logically relevant to the determination of a proposition's truth-value. It is whatever we must weigh, consider, observe, experience, or examine in order to render an informed verdict regarding a given proposition." What must we weigh and examine in order to verify Proposition

I.47? That would be Euclid's proof, of course, so the proof in this case is the evidence. Euclid's proof deduces I.47 from several prior propositions; those too are evidence. The prior propositions mentioned in the proof are logically relevant to the determination of I.47's truth-value, because if they are true, then I.47 must be true as well. We also examine Euclid's diagram—is that part of the evidence? Strictly speaking no, since the diagram is not logically relevant to the proof. It is merely a visual aid.

The prior propositions that Euclid employs in his proof of I.47 were themselves the subjects of proofs, proofs that cited yet earlier propositions. The chain of proofs would lead us back to the definitions, axioms, and postulates that appear at the beginning of Euclid's work. Although no proof or evidence is offered for them, none is needed. The definitions, axioms, and postulates that Euclid provides are just convenient assumptions. Technically they are neither true nor false. Taken as a group, Euclid's assumptions constitute the definition of Euclidean space. A Euclidean space, by definition, is just whatever satisfies Euclid's assumptions. Mathematicians can and do make other assumptions, to produce other types of space. Since the assumptions involved in these various geometric systems are not propositions, but rather definitional in nature, the demand for evidence does not apply to them. We can therefore accept the assumptions without evidence, yet not violate our evidentialist principles.

This distinction between propositions, which have truth-values, and definitions, which do not, is crucial to evidentialism. Though often misconstrued, the distinction ought to seem obvious once it is plainly spelled out.

Next, consider a simple perceptual belief, such as my belief that there is an Apple computer right in front of me at this very moment. What evidence is there for my belief? Well, what must be weighed, considered, observed, or experienced here? To determine that there is in fact an Apple computer present, the only thing I need to experience or observe is that computer, so the evidence for the existence of the computer is ... the computer! When it comes to evidential support for a belief, it cannot get any simpler than that. To say that a belief is supported by evidence is *not* to say that we necessarily arrive at the belief via some inference or argument. I do not, for example, infer the existence of the computer from sense data; neither do I persuade myself of the computer's existence by constructing an argument that employs as a premise some proposition regarding computerlike appearances. I just observe, and correctly identify, the computer.

"Could you not have identified it incorrectly," a skeptic might ask? "Could you not be suffering from an hallucination?" Of course I could. But evidentialism does not require that the evidence for our beliefs be infallible. Modest evidentialism permits us to use the fallible, corrigible, and possibly mistaken evidence that, in most instances, is all that will be available to us. Assume, though, that I am suffering from an hallucination. There is no Apple computer in front of me, so my belief that there is one is false. In this scenario, my belief enjoys no evidential support. The only evidence that a computer existed was the computer itself, but since that is gone, the evidence is gone too. So now I have two false beliefs: I believe falsely that there is a computer present; and I believe, equally incorrectly, that my first belief is evidentially supported. I have tried to proportion my belief to the evidence but failed. My belief in the computer is not justified, since it violates evidentialist canon. Am I justified? I do not think so. Granted, I did the best I could, and this should count in my favor. But doing one's best does not always get one off the hook. What if I were to run a red light, hit another car, and injure the driver? Perhaps I was doing the best I could; perhaps I only ran the light because I was tired and overworked or was distracted by some personal crisis (e.g., my girlfriend dumped me, or a family member had just passed away). Even so, the accident would be my fault, and I would be liable for any and all damages. The same reasoning applies to my beliefs about the computer. Perhaps I was doing my cognitive best. Still, I arrived at two false beliefs, not because the truth was especially difficult to discern, or because my environment was in some way misleading or ambiguous, but because of an hallucination manufactured by my own brain. I am at fault, even if I have not consciously or willingly done anything improper. Consequently, we cannot say that I am justified.

Our hypothetical skeptic might persist with his questions: "Surely you believe that the computer before you is not a hallucination. Where is the evidence for that belief?" No evidence suggests that my current experiences are hallucinatory; then again, I have no evidence, other than the computer, to prove that I am not hallucinating. The computer will not do as evidence, since its reality is the very thing in question. Although I could bring in a second person to verify my claim to have an Apple computer on my desk, our skeptic would not be satisfied with that witness's corroboration. How, he might ask, do I know that the second person isn't just another fictional character in my hallucination?

It might seem that at this point the evidence fails us and that only a leap of faith can bring me to the common sense view that my computer really exists. But I think that conclusion would be premature.

Evidentialism requires that we proportion belief to the evidence, so if no evidence supports either P or $\sim P$, an evidentialist will in most cases feel obliged to adopt the agnostic position. There are, however, exceptions to this agnostic rule. P and $\sim P$ may be epistemically unequal; one or the other of them may constitute the default position, which, in the absence of contrary evidence, we will rightly feel entitled to adopt. What breaks the tie between P and $\sim P$ is the application of some methodological rule or epistemological principle. The rule or principle in force creates the asymmetry between P and $\sim P$, and thereby determines which way our assent should go.

In the case at hand, my belief that I am not hallucinating is the proper default position. I am entitled to retain it until reasons emerge for doubting my senses. What makes this the default position? Philosophers call it the principle of credulity. This principle asserts our right to take the appearances at face value, at least provisionally. In effect, the principle holds that whatever looks like a duck, quacks like a duck, and waddles like a duck, should be taken for a duck, unless specific grounds for questioning that belief can be given. What goes for ducks, goes also for computers. Since there appears to be a computer in front of me, and since no specific grounds exist for doubting my senses, I may lawfully apply the credulity principle by believing in the computer's reality. Had I "seen" Bigfoot, or little green men from outer space, that would be different; there are legitimate grounds for doubting the existence of those things. Yet my Apple computer is hardly on a par with Bigfoot. The bare logical possibility that the computer *might* be an hallucination provides no specific grounds for thinking that it *is* one, so skepticism on the issue is not warranted.

"And where," someone might ask, "is the evidence for this credulity principle?" Although there is no evidence for the credulity principle, none is needed. The credulity principle is one of a number of principles that philosophers sometimes refer to as the necessary presuppositions of rational inquiry. We really have no choice but to accept these. Even the most radical of skeptics must take such principles entirely for granted throughout his reflections. When the skeptic expresses his doubts concerning some proposition, he must use words to do so. How does he know what those words mean, unless he assumes that they mean what they appear to him to mean? How does he know he doubts, unless the appearance of doubting is taken without question to be veridical? The credulity principle is thus not optional, not even for the most determined skeptic; he cannot abandon that principle, or any of its cousins, without committing intellectual suicide.

If the credulity principle is not optional, neither is it true. It is simply an assumption whose protected status is guaranteed by the simple fact that without it intelligible thought cannot occur. The credulity principle, and various others of a like nature, collectively constitute the definition of rational inquiry. By definition, rational inquiry is just whatever gets done under the aegis of those assumptions. The necessary presuppositions of rational inquiry thus bear some analogy to the axioms of Euclid. Presuppositions such as the credulity principle are to rationality what Euclid's axioms are to his geometry. The difference, of course, is that while there can be many geometric systems, there can be only one universal standard of rationality.

Although the claim that a universal standard of rationality exists might seem a bold one, it is really nothing more than a tautology. Any principle that is not universally obligatory (in the same sense in which the credulity principle is obligatory) is for that very reason disqualified from being a *necessary* presupposition. It automatically follows that there can be one and only one set of such presuppositions. Rationality therefore cannot be fragmented into different varieties, the way geometry fragments into different geometric systems.

Belief should be proportioned to the evidence—this was said before, many times. What was not said earlier is that belief should also be proportioned to the way an hypothesis obeys those presuppositions of rational inquiry just mentioned. No contradiction or conflict results from this addition. Just as, in physics, force can be proportional to both mass and acceleration, so in philosophy, we may proportion belief both to the evidence and to degree of conformity with our epistemic principles.

Next, consider a memory belief, such as my belief that I once lived in Connecticut. I believe that I lived in Connecticut because I remember being there years ago, yet the memory is not the evidence for my belief, any more than my perceptions are the evidence for my belief that I own an IMac. The evidence for my memory beliefs, like the evidence for my perceptual beliefs, consists of whatever real objects I observed, together with the real events I experienced or in which I participated. The events, of course, are over; many of the objects have disappeared. Buildings have been torn down, documents lost, and so on. The evidence—much of it, anyway—is no longer available for review. Yet that does not matter. The evidence was there when I needed it. I formed my beliefs about Connecticut appropriately, and in accordance with such evidence as was available at the time. I need not abandon those beliefs simply because the evidence for them has faded away. So if evidentialism requires us to proportion belief to the evidence, this should not be interpreted to mean that the evidence must always remain at our fingertips. It suffices if the evidence was once at our fingertips.

Finally, let us examine my belief that there is such a place as Australia. Although I have never been there, I have heard much about it. I have inferred the existence of Australia from maps and atlases, news reports, and travelers' testimony. Those things are my evidence. As with many of my memory beliefs, the original evidence for my belief in Australia has faded into obscurity. I no longer even remember what maps I consulted, or who I spoke to, or what news broadcasts might have been the first to mention Australia in my presence. Once again, though, none of that matters. The evidence that Australia exists is overwhelming; the portion of it to which I personally have been exposed represents only a tiny fraction of what is actually available. If I needed to, perhaps to persuade a skeptic, I could marshal as much evidence for the existence of Australia as I pleased. I could even put that skeptic on the next Quantas flight to Sidney with instructions to send me a postcard after he landed. It thus seems reasonable to say that what justifies my confidently held belief in Australia is not merely the snippets of evidence I might happen to have encountered, but also all the other evidence for Australia to which I have access, and which I know to be out there. The same principle applies to my belief in the big bang; the evidence for that belief is not just whatever I might have read about that event—it is instead the whole body of relevant and publicly available research performed by members of the scientific community. Sometimes, then, it is not even necessary that the evidence to which my belief gets proportioned have been once at my fingertips. In certain circumstances at least, it suffices if the evidence exists, and I can either put my fingertips on it when I need to, or else tell someone else where to find it.

Some authors have claimed that beliefs about elements of common knowledge, such as my belief in Australia, are not based on evidence. They support this paradoxical thesis by citing a valid rule of argument. The premises of any argument, they note, must be better known than the conclusion. Suppose I want to persuade you that P is the case, and I put forth Q, R, S, and T as the evidence for P. My argument will work only if you are willing to accept Q, R, S, and T. But if from your perspective those other propositions are just as open to doubt and uncertainty as P, then you will reject my argument, and rightly so. The existence of Australia, say these authors, is so firmly established that we actually have more confidence in it, than we do in any particular piece of evidence that might be adduced for it. We trust that Australia exists more than we trust the honesty of any one traveler, or the accuracy of any one news report or purported map. Were we to encounter a map of the Pacific that left Australia out, we would question the competence of the mapmaker, not the reality of the continent. Therefore, they say, we cannot construct a valid argument for the existence of Australia, which entails that our belief in that place cannot be based on the evidence.

When we arrive by apparently valid steps of reasoning at a conclusion that is obviously nonsensical, we ought to go back and check our premises, to see where we went wrong. That my belief in Australia is devoid of evidential support is obvious nonsense; said belief enjoys massive evidential support. How else could the belief have become so firmly established? What, other than the ready availability of overwhelming and convincing evidence, could have established the fact in question, and made it a piece of common knowledge?

Clearly the commentators alluded to have erred somewhere. I believe their mistake lies in confusing the logic of persuasion with the logic of belief justification. The rule of argument cited above concerns the logic of persuasion; it only applies when we are trying to convince someone. The rule merely explains that persuasion is a matter of leading our listener from the known to the unknown. This has nothing at all to do with belief justification. My belief in Australia is justified by the evidence; it can be justified in no other way. Were I to construct an argument for Australia's existence, it would be a cogent inductive argument; it would justify my belief, and perhaps also suffice to convince any reasonable skeptic. If the argument is not in the right format to convince me (because of the rule of argument cited), that is irrelevant, for I am convinced already. Furthermore, I was originally convinced by evidence of the very same kind contained in my argument. The argument would thus explain why my conviction about Australia is so strong. What more could be required to show that my belief in Australia is proportioned to the evidence?

Think of a building supported by a thousand pillars. An edifice so firmly grounded is probably more stable than any one of its pillars. In the event of an earthquake, the building would stand firm, even if a few of the pillars collapsed. Yet the building still depends on those pillars, since obviously it cannot float in midair. Likewise with my belief in Australia—the fact of Australia's existence is better known to me than any of the thousands of bits of evidence connected to it, yet it does not follow that my belief now hovers unsupported in the middle of some cognitive space. My belief still depends on the evidence, since it is the evidence that made the fact in question so well known.

Section 21

INTUITION

The evidence upon which we base our beliefs does not always, or even usually, boil down to anything that might be said to exist within our minds. In paradigmatic cases, the bedrock for our perceptual beliefs, memory beliefs, and scientific or historical beliefs rests upon items in the public domain. Sometimes, though, the evidence for a belief may consist of private phenomena, such as an intuition, sensation, or feeling. The belief is not necessarily worse off for that.

Think about thermometers. A thermometer contains a column of mercury, which rises or falls in accordance with changes in air temperature. Although a thermometer has no idea what it is doing, it does not need to. The data it provides is still good evidence for the ambient temperature. Similarly, if I have a gut feeling that someone is lying to me, that may be solid evidence of his or her deceitfulness. I need not understand the mechanisms that activate such gut reactions; neither must I be able to articulate what provoked the feeling in this particular case. If the lie-detection software built into my brain normally gives reliable clues to other people's dishonesty, then the gut feelings that result count as evidence.

The reliability of my gut feelings is subject to independent third-party testing. If I am a competent discerner of lies, then it should be possible, at least in principle, to prove that competence to open-minded skeptics. But I am not obligated to wait for such confirmation. Even if my abilities are never scientifically tested, my beliefs concerning liars will be justified, provided that I do have the cognitive competence in question. Nonetheless, we ought to exercise some skeptical caution when making presumptions regarding our own cognitive faculties. Sometimes our "gut feelings" represent nothing more than guesswork, and what we proudly describe as "intuitions" are just so many thoughtless prejudices.

Section 22

THE OBVIOUS

One class of beliefs not yet touched on has to do with things that seem obvious. Consider simple propositions such as "The whole is greater than the part," "All beautiful women over five feet tall are female," or "Two is half of four." They are obviously true, but what evidence do we have for their truth? They are their own evidence. In each case the only evidence we need for the proposition is the proposition itself. That is why such propositions are often referred to as being self-evident.

Some philosophers have thought this improper. A proposition, they say, cannot be evidence for itself, any more than a witness can corroborate his own testimony. Certainly a witness cannot corroborate his own testimony when he testifies to the occurrence of some event distant in time and place, but what if the witness is testifying to the fact that he, the witness, speaks English? If he delivers his testimony in complete, grammatical English sentences, then his testimony does to a very large extent corroborate itself. To discover the truth of what he says, we need do no more than listen to what he says. The situation is similar with self-evident propositions. To discover the truth of a self-evident proposition, we need look no further than the contents of the proposition itself. If evidence is just whatever we must weigh, consider, or examine in order to correctly appraise the truth-value of a proposition, then clearly the evidence for a given proposition P will sometimes be nothing other than P itself.

Section 23

KNOWLEDGE

Ever since Plato, philosophers have wanted to distinguish between knowledge and true belief. Given this objective, the question becomes: What must we add to true belief to make it knowledge? Twenty-four centuries of philosophical argument have not yielded a definitive answer; there is no general agreement as to what must be added, or even what to call it. Consider this definition of "knowledge" as our provisional account:

> Simple epistemic functionalism: A belief counts as "knowledge" if it is true, and if it is held confidently enough to be employed without hesitation in all endeavors, whether practical or theoretical.

I call this a functionalist account of knowledge because it focuses not on the credentials of knowledge—where and how one obtained it or from whom—but rather on what one is willing and able to do with it. On this view, knowledge is just accurate and useful information. With regard to knowledge functionalism, ask the engineer's question: Does it work? The assumption is that whatever does the job of knowledge is knowledge. Something other than knowledge might on occasion mimic knowledge; but if in every situation the stuff stored in our brains performs exactly the way knowledge would, that is not mimicry. It is the real McCoy.

Simple epistemic functionalism accords well with our ordinary conversational use of the word "knowledge." In many cases, at least, when we say that we know something, we mean only that it is in fact true, that we confidently believe it to be so, and that we feel we can put our trust in it. We are, in addition, often telling others that they can trust it too. We are passing our knowledge on to them.

Simple epistemic functionalism makes it easy to determine when knowledge is present. Suppose we want to find out what a certain engineering student knows about Newtonian mechanics. All we have to do is pose the right questions. We might ask the student to write down Newton's equations for us, explain what the terms in the equations mean, and solve a few problems using those equations. If the student passes our test, then he obviously knows something about mechanics. But if the student gets several questions wrong, frequently hesitates when answering, or takes a very long time to solve the simplest problems, then we might conclude that he doesn't really know very much. Perhaps some of his correct answers were just good guesses.

Given the ready testability of knowledge as defined by simple epistemic functionalism, it might be fair to say that functionalist knowledge is the only kind of knowledge one needs in order to get good grades in school. Such knowledge will also pass muster in most other places. However, if simple epistemic functionalism were all there were to knowledge, then twenty-four centuries of philosophical debate have been conducted in vain. We should therefore suspect that there must be more to knowledge than what we have identified so far. In short, simple epistemic functionalism is probably too simple.

A widely recognized characteristic of knowledge is that it is hard, in the technical sense of "hard" presented in the first section of this essay. Consider again my knowledge of Australia.

I do *know* that there is such a place. Knowing that, rather than merely believing it, implies (among other things) that I can use this information as a background against which other factual claims can be tested for plausibility. Were a traveler to tell me that he had surveyed the southwestern Pacific and found Australia to be missing, I would not take this as any disconfirmation of Australia's existence; instead I would take it as proof either that this so-called traveler was lying or that he had gotten lost at sea and did not know where he had been. Our engineering student's beliefs about Newtonian mechanics must display a similar resilience if they are to count as knowledge. Suppose, for example, that the student were to build a model airplane, only to see it crash immediately during its first flight. If he knows that his equations are correct, then the crash will not cause him to question their validity. Instead he will assume that he miscalculated somewhere, and he will recheck his figures. Knowledge, then, requires not just confidence of belief but a confidence that is not easily shaken.

If knowledge must be hard, it is also important that it not be too hard. An absolutely invincible confidence in some purported truth may be a sign not of knowledge but of a belief held on faith—one might say blind faith. But how do we distinguish the hardness appropriate to knowledge from that which is symptomatic of faith? One way to describe the distinction is to say that knowledge is not just hard; it is, in a sense, also *brittle*. Given some proposition P, a hard belief that P becomes "brittle" when the believer is open-minded enough to recognize, and be responsive to, any and all future circumstances that might suffice to cast doubt on P. Sometimes, of course, there are no such circumstances. What circumstances would suffice to cast doubt on our belief that $2 + 1 = 3$? More often, though, such circumstances are at least theoretically possible. Even our best established bits of apparent knowledge are normally subject in principle to further examination and revision. When that is the case, the knower should have some grasp of how it would work.

We can now upgrade our earlier definition of knowledge. This will make the conditions of knowledge much stricter:

> Epistemic functionalism 2.0: For any proposition *P* and mind *M*, *M* knows that *P* if (a) *P* is true, (b) *M* believes that *P*, (c) *M* is confident enough in *P* to employ it in all endeavors, whether practical or theoretical, and (d) *M* understands both how to use *P* to test the plausibility of other factual claims, and how to test *P* itself, in situations where *P*'s truth might be legitimately open to question.

Epistemic functionalism sees knowledge as a kind of skill; to know that *P* is both to possess the information that *P* contains, and to be able to use that information effectively, within the limits imposed by one's other cognitive and physical abilities. In short, knowledge is defined in terms of the effect knowledge has on know-how. For the upgraded version of functionalism, knowing how to work with knowledge includes knowing when to reject it, and when to reject other things because of it. To that extent, upgraded epistemic functionalism presents a fallibilistic view of knowledge.

Can we now conclude that knowledge is just what our upgraded epistemic functionalism says it is? Sadly, no. We have yet to ask the philosopher's question: Is it good? The correct answer, I think, is that while functionalist knowledge is pretty good, it is not good enough. Even functionalism 2.0 still ignores the credentials of knowledge: the where, when, how, and from whence of knowledge. Credentials do matter.

Suppose for the sake of argument that Pascal was right, and that reason alone can incline the mind neither to theism, nor to atheism. Suppose further that a man who is aware of this persistent inconclusiveness of the evidence decides to take

Pascal's Wager and believe in the God of Roman Catholicism. He comes to enjoy a firm religious conviction; he employs his faith in matters both theoretical and practical; his belief displays adequate levels of hardness, yet it is also brittle, since, if evidence against it were to arise, he would be responsive to that. Should God actually exist, then the man's theism would pass the functionalist test for knowledge. But would it be knowledge, even then? We might well have qualms about that. Pascal's Wager is not a method of knowledge acquisition, only a strategy for playing a high-stakes guessing game. Taking the wager does not imply that one knows God to exist, any more than betting on Philosopher's Folly in the fifth implies that one knows the horse will win. Even if Philosopher's Folly does win, and even if a gambler had total confidence in that, he did not necessarily know the race's outcome ahead of time. He might just have made a lucky guess, and then built up his confidence through self-deception. Likewise with the theist—his lucky guess, combined with self-deception, would not amount to knowledge.

Now think of the jury at a murder trial. The crime was an especially grisly event. In this jurisdiction, the defendant will face the death penalty if convicted. With a man's life at stake, the jury cannot in good conscience turn in a guilty verdict unless they know for a fact that the defendant committed murder. They must be sure, and their confidence cannot be just a matter of subjective certainty. Evidence must exist to back it up. The evidence needs to justify belief beyond a reasonable doubt. Here it seems very clear that the credentials of belief have become crucial. To vote for guilt, the jury requires more than a merely functionalist version of knowledge; at a minimum, they require that, plus justification for both themselves and their beliefs.

After reflecting on Pascal's Wager and the hypothetical murder trial, we ought to conclude that knowledge is not genuine unless it is justified. "Unjustified knowledge" seems like an oxymoron. The sentence "I know that *P* is true but I have no grounds for thinking it to be so" is at best paradoxical. Unfortunately, we cannot content ourselves with the addition of a justification clause to the definition of knowledge. This maneuver is defeated by what the philosophical literature refers to as Gettier scenarios. Here is the classic case: a man named Smith tells you that he owns a Ford. He shows you the bill of sale, the title, and so on. On that evidence, you come to believe that Smith owns a Ford. You decide further to accept belief in the proposition "Smith owns a Ford or Brown is in Barcelona," Mr. Brown being a friend concerning whose location you have no information. If Smith does own a Ford, then "Smith owns a Ford or Brown is in Barcelona" will be true, so you have just as much evidence for this second belief as you did for the first. Now suppose Smith was lying: he does not really own a car at all; yet by chance Brown just happens to be in Barcelona. Although your second belief, the one concerning both Smith and Brown, is true, and justified, and perhaps very confidently held, our intuitions suggest that it should not count as knowledge. Your belief about Smith and Brown lacks appropriate credentials, because it was based on a lie (plus a fortuitous coincidence).

All of the Gettier scenarios play upon this same theme. They all involve situations where the evidence that justifies some belief suffers from some form of corruption. Think again of the jurors at the murder trial. Imagine that the defendant really is guilty and that the jurors come to believe in his guilt based upon what they very reasonably take to be overwhelming evidence. Imagine though, that unbeknownst to them, the evidence presented at trial was misleading, falsified, or in some other way illicit. Key witnesses lied; the DNA sample was contaminated; the detectives broke their department's chain of custody policies while transporting the murder weapon; the voice recognition software used to analyze the 911 tapes was unreliable and based on junk science; the defendant's confession was beaten out of him, and he was not Mirandized. Very minor procedural glitches will not invalidate the jury's claim to know that the defendant is guilty. Other, more serious, flaws in the evidence, however, would compromise that claim. It would thus appear that the evidence upon which knowledge is based must be, if not perfect, at least free from serious flaws. How serious does a flaw have to be to void a knowledge claim? There may not be any firm rule for that. The decision requires a judgment call, to be made on a case-by-case basis.

We can question the competency of the jurors as well as that of the prosecutors and detectives. Did the jury evaluate the evidence responsibly? Did they permit their passional natures to influence their judgment? Did any of them suffer from hallucinations during the trial, perhaps hearing the voices of imaginary witnesses? Method, as I have said before, is everything, so any flaws in the jury's perception of the evidence, or in their assumptions about it, or in their attitudes toward it, will speak to the credibility of their decision.

Let us say that a belief is *fully functional* if it meets all of the criteria for knowledge laid down by epistemic functionalism 2.0, including, of course, the requirement that the belief be true. Let us further stipulate that a belief is *properly grounded* if it is justified, and the evidence involved (including any supporting arguments) is of adequate quality. Finally, we should say that a belief is *fairly held* if the believer has weighed the evidence without undue illusion or bias, and in a manner relatively free of other methodological faults. The range of potential faults is great, so once again we cannot specify all conditions but must leave something to case-by-case judgment. This permits us to offer the following very succinct definition of knowledge:

> Evidential functionalism: a belief counts as knowledge if and only if it is fully functional, properly grounded, and fairly held.

This definition of knowledge seems compatible with ordinary English usage. In addition, it gives voice to the perennial craving of philosophers, who have long wanted the word "knowledge" to stand for something special, and who consequently have sought to create this special object of desire by attaching to true belief some extra badge of honor, or certificate of authenticity, or even a blue ribbon for cognitive achievement.

Section 24

WARRANT

Alvin Plantinga gives an account of knowledge very different from the one I offered in the preceding section. Knowledge, he says, is warranted true belief. It is warrant, then, that must be added to true belief to make it knowledge. At least we now have a name for that blue ribbon of cognitive achievement that identifies knowledge as knowledge. In conversational English, the term "warranted" is often used interchangeably with "justified"; for Plantinga, however, warrant and justification are entirely separate concepts. Warrant is the star of his epistemology. Justification is demoted to insignificance. Plantinga describes "warrant" as follows:

> A belief has warrant just if it is produced by cognitive processes or faculties that are functioning properly, in a cognitive environment that is propitious for that exercise of cognitive powers, according to a design plan that is successfully aimed at the production of true belief.[xxviii]

The focus on warrant instead of justification removes the concept of evidence from the knowledge equation. Plantinga is not an evidentialist. In fact, he is vehemently opposed to evidentialism. Of course, this anti-evidentialism fades immediately into the background whenever Plantinga thinks he has evidence for his beliefs, and also when he is criticizing his opponents' beliefs for their lack of evidential support. On all such occasions, he becomes an excellent evidentialist. But at least in theory Plantinga holds to the view that evidence has very little to do with human cognition. His entire epistemology is geared to prove that knowledge does not depend on evidence. This is all part of his larger program for defending Christianity.

Plantinga calls his epistemology "naturalistic." This is highly misleading. Plantinga does not believe that there is any viable, purely naturalistic account of knowledge. His conceptions of proper function and design are laced with theistic presuppositions. In *Warrant and Proper Function*, he argues that a naturalistic epistemology can only work in the context of a supernaturalist metaphysics. Of course, once we introduce the metaphysics of theism to explain the conceptual foundations of naturalistic epistemology, then that epistemology is naturalistic no longer. What Plantinga really means, then, is that naturalistic epistemology is doomed to failure, and should be replaced by supernaturalistic epistemology. One wishes that he had said that more openly.

By describing his views as "naturalistic," Plantinga intends to contrast them with deontological perspectives on knowledge. A deontological epistemology is basically one that takes seriously the concept of there being such a thing as an ethics of belief. Plantinga rejects that concept. He is willing to say that in certain situations there is something one ought to believe. Yet this "ought" has no ethical significance. It is the same "ought" we employ when we say that a human heart ought to pump blood, or that a car engine ought to start when the ignition is turned. From this perspective, what the human mind ought to do is neither more nor less than what it is designed to do—what, in other words, it actually does do when it is functioning properly and not malfunctioning, using all these terms in exactly the same way an engineer would. To Plantinga, this makes perfect sense, since the engineer who designed us is God.

The question "What is knowledge?" does not necessarily yield just one right answer. It is possible, at least in principle, for there to be multiple definitions of knowledge, differing widely from one another, yet all equally coherent and defensible. With regard to any given definition of knowledge, the issue is not "Is it true?" for definitions have no truth-values. The issue instead is "Does it work?" Plantinga's conception of knowledge does not work. It is what I would call a paper bridge. Plantinga wants to cross this bridge into Christian faith, but it cannot support the weight he needs to put on it. The bridge collapses quickly upon inspection.

How can God know anything, we should ask, if knowledge is what Plantinga claims it is? God has no design plan. Even if there is some sense in which God displays order, the order implicit in the divine nature cannot be a designed order. This would appear to prevent God from ever having knowledge in Plantinga's sense.

Think of a rock worn smooth in a stream. It has no design plan, only a pleasing shape. I pick it up and decide to use it to pound nails into a board. The rock now has a purpose but still no design. The rock does not acquire a design until I modify it in some way. Perhaps I chip off a few flakes to create a gripping surface or file away a notch useful for pulling nails out of the wood. Once modified, the rock is no longer just a rock, but a makeshift hammer, with a design conferred upon it by its designer, namely me. Designed objects are those made for a purpose; they have been created or modified with that purpose in view. For a designed object, the purpose explains the structure. The object has that structure because it is intended to achieve that purpose. Nothing like this can be the case with God. No person or process designed God; no design work went into his creation, because he was not created. Since God is eternal, it seems reasonable to suppose that he has never even been modified. His original perfection remains intact. God may have a purpose, but since that purpose did not become causally involved in producing the divine order, God cannot be said to have a design plan, or to be a designed being. So even when God's cognitive faculties are functioning marvelously well (which, we must assume, is always the case), still they are not functioning according to a design plan aimed at truth, as Plantinga's definition of knowledge requires. It seems, then, that contrary to popular belief, God is not omniscient. In fact, given Plantinga's definition of knowledge, God knows nothing at all, since there is no design plan to confer warrant on his infinite stock of true beliefs. A God devoid of knowledge is not what Plantinga wished to produce; nor is it anything his fellow Christians would wish to worship. But this is the God that Plantinga's epistemology forces upon him.

I do not see how Planting might fix this problem. He cannot, for example, simply declare that God designs himself. Design plans are essentially forward looking. They provide programs for action. One cannot plan the present or the past, but only record them. But since God exists in an eternal present, he has no future for which to plan. Any "plan" he drew up for himself would only record the way he already is, and so would not be a true plan at all. There thus seems no way for Plantinga to get around the nasty conclusion that his God is undesigned and, consequently, bereft of knowledge.

The same problem arises if we consider gods other than the Christian God. Suppose the world were run by the Homeric deities. The gods described in Homer's *Iliad* are clearly intelligent beings capable of knowledge; equally clearly, they are not the products of design. They are no one's artifacts. So how would Plantinga account for them? A denial of the existence of Zeus, Athena, and Apollo will not suffice. Any legitimate definition of knowledge should be able to say what knowledge is for any intelligent being in any possible world, not just what it is for some specific subclass of beings in some favored world.

The question of animal knowledge leads to another difficulty. It seems natural to attribute some knowledge to nonhuman creatures. My cat Mikey, for example, knows where his food bowl is: it is in the kitchen. There is no problem incorporating this idea into the knowledge scheme I have presented. Mikey does not consider any arguments when weighing possible beliefs. His poor verbal skills prevent him from doing that. In other respects, though, his belief acquisition differs little from the way in which humans acquire their most elementary beliefs connected to perception and memory. Mikey's belief that his food bowl is in the kitchen seems to me more than sufficiently functional, grounded, and fair.

Although Plantinga does not discuss animal knowledge anywhere that I know of, I think he would agree with me that Mikey possesses knowledge. God, he would say, has successfully aimed the cognitive design plans of higher animals at the acquisition of such true beliefs as are appropriate to their station in life. There is some plausibility to this. If there was a God, maybe he would design the cognitive structures of certain animals for the purpose of truth discovery. But suppose this were not the case. Suppose God communicated to us that he designed animal neural systems for the sole purpose of guiding their behavior. He wanted to make sure that cats could find mice, avoid predators, and so on. The production of true beliefs was just an accidental by-product of that behavioral objective, in much the way heat is an accidental by-product of the operation of a car's internal combustion engine, or the "thumpa thumpa" sound made by a human heart is an accidental by-product of its effort to pump blood. Plantinga's theory of design allows for the existence of accidental by-products; the examples I have given of that phenomenon are his own. Now if God did tell us that the production of true beliefs in animals was accidental relative to his divine plans (albeit an entirely foreseeable accident), then Plantinga should feel obliged to say that Mikey and other nonhuman creatures know nothing. His definition of knowledge would prohibit them from obtaining knowledge, so the most they could enjoy would be true belief.

This result seems wildly counterintuitive. How can some feature of a design plan laid up in heaven make the difference between knowledge and true belief here on earth? Surely that difference in Mikey's case has to do with the cognitive transaction between him and his food bowl, and with that alone? If Plantinga sticks to his guns on this issue, he must then admit that the question "Does Mikey know things?" is one we can never answer, since in practice we never do get the crucial insights from God concerning his plans. We cannot peer into God's mind to see if Mikey gets his blue ribbon.

A counterintuitive result is not always fatal to a theory. If a theory is sufficiently attractive in other respects, and provides a simple and compelling account of the phenomena, we might prefer to reeducate our intuitions rather than change (and perhaps complicate) our theory. Yet Plantinga does say that his goal is to analyze our common-sense notion of knowledge to see what it involves. Conclusions such as those just discussed, which run against common sense, severely weaken the plausibility of his epistemology.

Given these reflections on gods and animals, the right conclusion would appear to be this one: knowledge depends on the possession of cognitive skills. Mikey knows things because he has the skills necessary to learn them. We can therefore know that he knows them, without needing to ask whether he was designed for the purpose of learning them. The same idea applies to God: if he exists then he knows everything because his infinite cognitive skill set permits him to know all. That he has no design plan matters not. Design plans, then, are simply irrelevant to knowledge. Plantinga's reliance on that concept for the construction of his epistemology would appear to have been misguided.

Now let us turn our attention to human knowledge. More specifically, let us look at *a priori* knowledge, to which Plantinga devotes an entire chapter of *Warrant and Proper Function*. Imagine that we have discovered a new theorem in Euclidean geometry, and that we have spelled out a cogent proof of it. What warrants our discovery and makes it knowledge, rather than, say, a lucky guess? If the theorem is not something obvious to intuition, then any warrant it enjoys must lie in the proof. So what makes the proof cogent? The only answer that comes to mind is: the rules of logic. Reasoning is a rule-based activity. To reason soundly is to apply logical principles correctly; fallacious reasoning involves flouting those principles or applying them incorrectly. Reasoning is judged by the rules of logic, in exactly the same sense in which speech is judged by the rules of grammar. The difference, of course, is that the rules of grammar are largely arbitrary, and may differ greatly from one language to another. Fundamental logical rules are not arbitrary. If we encountered beings from another planet, Klingons, say, or Vulcans, or people from Alpha Centauri, we would expect them to recognize pretty much the same logical rules we do. If they did not, we would be unable to translate their languages into our own; we would not even be able to recognize them as rational creatures like ourselves.

The rules of logic specify what follows from what, and thus, what we may or may not permissibly infer. In a word, the rules tell us how we ought to think. This use of "ought," however, is not the engineer's. It is an entirely different, and thoroughly deontological, "ought." To say, as an engineer would, that a car's engine ought to start when the ignition is turned, is simply to say the car is designed to work that way. The "oughts" of a car are determined by its design plan, just as Plantinga says. The "oughts" of logic do not derive from any design plan. Just the opposite: the design plan for our logical faculties would have to be based upon the rules of logic. Those rules would determine whether any particular design plan was a good one, in the sense of being successfully aimed at the production of true belief. They would also determine whether, in any given situation, our cognitive faculties were functioning properly. A malfunction in our logical faculty can only be identified by a failure to follow the rules of clear thinking.

This is fatal for Plantinga's outlook. His theory of knowledge depends on the distinctions between good and bad design, and between function and malfunction. Yet making those distinctions correctly requires an appeal to deontological rules that, according to his theory, do not exist. Plantinga has no viable options here. If he says that there are no logical rules we ought to follow, then he is saying something obviously absurd. Can he claim instead that logical rules exist, but that they are merely arbitrary habits ingrained into human nature by God? In that case, God could have designed our habits completely differently. How, one wonders, would this work? I do not see how anything like that would be possible. What kind of "logic" would reject *modus ponens*, and put its signature of approval on everything we currently consider fallacious? Does that make any sense at all? How can we even decide what makes sense without relying on the rules of logic we already have? But should Plantinga concede that logic is neither God's invention nor a queer idiosyncrasy of mankind, this opens the door to the deontological epistemology he has worked so hard to avoid. Nor is Plantinga's problem here confined to mathematics. Our inductive reasoning concerning empirical issues also follows rules, and these are equally difficult to reduce to merely human conventions. To banish the credulity principle, or Occam's razor, entirely from our thoughts would appear just as fantastic as abandoning *modus ponens*. If Plantinga thinks he can throw out all such principles, create new ones from scratch, and imagine another rational species operating under those new principles, then he owes us an account of the matter. This would seem impossible, though, for in describing the new principles, he would constantly have to appeal to the old ones.

Section 25

THE FOOTNOTE

On the second to last page of *Warrant and Proper Function*, buried in a footnote, Plantinga addresses the issue of God's knowledge. Although God does not have a design plan, Plantinga concedes, we can nonetheless apply the concept of knowledge to him by analogy. God's cognitive faculties obviously work well—perfectly, in fact, since God is omniscient. So let the way God's mind works be represented by the symbol W. Plantinga postulates a set that puts all cognitive design plans in order, from worst to best; he then adds W to that ordered set, as its final member. God's cognitive system, Plantinga tells us, is related to other such systems by being their ideal. We extend the concept of knowledge to him in virtue of that relationship.

Plantinga's response here seems both tortured and clueless. By what right do we add something that is not a design plan to a set that puts all design plans in a certain order? How can it be a member of that set? Are we to imagine W as the design plan God would have, if a still higher God had created him? To even suggest that is to throw away the notion that God is a necessary being, a notion upon which Plantinga insists in that same footnote.

If God existed, he would no doubt represent the ideal in cognitive excellence. In saying that, however, we are already assuming that God possesses knowledge, that he knows all, and knows it in a way that is even more excellent than our way. Plantinga cannot embed that assumption within an argument purporting to establish the thesis that we can apply the knowledge concept to God, for then Plantinga would be assuming the very thing to be proven, and thus be reasoning in a circle. If we remove the assumption in question, we are left with a God who perhaps has true beliefs about everything but apparently no knowledge of anything. How can that God be the ultimate cognitive ideal?

Let us grant for the sake of argument that God does have an infinite and complete stock of true beliefs. We are still entitled to ask the same question about those beliefs that we ask about our own, namely, what must get added to them to make them knowledge? It cannot be warrant, as Plantinga defines the term. What is it, then?

Suppose Plantinga answers this question by eliminating the design concept from his definition of warrant. He could then say that God possesses knowledge via the proper functioning of his infinite cognitive faculties within the supremely propitious environment of heaven. This approach would obligate Plantinga to explain what proper functioning means, given that he can no longer define the term by referring to design plans or designers. If he fails to accomplish that task, his epistemology will be ruined. If, on the other hand, he succeeds, he thereby undermines one of his arguments against atheism. That argument held atheism to be indefensible, because there clearly is such a thing as the proper functioning of the human mind, and because there is no viable, purely naturalistic way to account for that without appealing to the designs of a conscious, intelligent creator. But if Plantinga can handle the concepts of knowledge and proper functioning without such appeals, why cannot any atheist do likewise? Plantinga might decide to do without the concept of proper functioning; however, should he go that route, nothing of any substance would remain from his initial definition of warrant. His entire epistemology would be gutted.

Section 26

TIGERS

Plantinga offers a second argument that purports to demonstrate the irrationality of atheism. It is far more interesting than the one mentioned in section 25, and more complicated too. But a careful analysis will show it to have no more plausibility than the first.

Assume that there is no God, and that mankind's cognitive faculties emerged through the mechanisms of Darwinian evolution. Under these conditions, we can still be said to have both a design plan and a designer. Our designer would be natural selection. That is the primary driving force behind the evolutionary process. Over the course of millions of years, natural selection will have molded us into our current form. Our bones, muscles, nervous systems, and cognitive faculties would all be the result of its handiwork. Our design plan would then consist of all the traits that got selected for during our species's evolutionary history.

The problem, or apparent problem, with this atheistic scenario is that natural selection has no reason to care about truth. It does not literally care about anything, but even if we permit ourselves to speak metaphorically, it seems that selection only "cares" about behavior. It selects for those cognitive structures that generate adaptive behavior. Whatever cognitive structures happen to promote survival and reproduction will be the ones natural selection "likes" best. Natural selection could, of course, produce a species exactly like our own, a large brained, highly intelligent species whose members could perform all of the overt actions we do. They could talk, make sophisticated tools, form complex social groups, build skyscrapers, compose symphonies, and so on. At least there are no *a priori* grounds for supposing that natural selection could not do exactly that. Perhaps it could even be expected to do that. Yet what assurance do we have that the creatures so produced would arrive at mostly true beliefs? The design plan for these animals would be aimed at adaptive behavior, not truth, so relative to that design plan, any true beliefs the animals adopted would be merely the accidental by-products of their cognitive functioning. But if true beliefs could be accidents, then so too could false beliefs. This raises the suspicion that evolution might create a species whose outwardly intelligent behavior was accompanied by mostly false beliefs. So how do we know that we are not just such a chronically deluded species?

We can easily imagine cases where a given piece of adaptive behavior might emerge from either true beliefs or false ones. Suppose that one of our hominid ancestors saw a tiger prowling across the African savanna. The hominid might believe that he had seen a tiger, believe that tigers are dangerous, and so run away, thus saving himself from being eaten. Here adaptive behavior emerges from true belief. But suppose the hominid incorrectly identifies the tiger as a banana tree. Believing that bananas are always poisonous, he runs off in the other direction, still saving himself from the undetected tiger. This time the adaptive behavior comes from a concatenation of mostly false beliefs.

Obviously, then, two or more false beliefs might accidentally get conjoined so as to elicit from their owner some prudent act. It could happen once, twice, maybe even three times in succession. Could it happen all the time, or even most of the time? Could every member of a large and diverse species see this same kind of "accident" occur over and over again, in many different environments, throughout the course of centuries? That would be like throwing a pair of dice and getting snake eyes billions of times in a row. The probability of such a thing occurring is, for all intents and purposes, zero. Nor could natural selection arrange for events to unfold in the manner this scenario requires. Artfully orchestrating the production of false beliefs, which then consistently—and one might say magically—cancel each other out in just the right way (almost) every time, would be impossible.

We are thus forced to conclude that while the hominid who cannot tell tigers from banana trees might get lucky today, sooner or later he will either starve to death or get eaten, guaranteed. To preserve any hope of long-term survival, that hominid will need mostly true beliefs. So even if true belief is in one sense an accidental by-product of our design plan, in another sense it is no accident. Evolution cannot avoid endowing us with a propensity to form mostly true beliefs on many issues, any more than an engineer in Detroit can avoid endowing internal combustion engines with a propensity to consume energy.

The conclusion of the last paragraph follows only if we assume a normal connection between beliefs and overt actions. Plantinga, however, argues that Darwinian processes might lead to the emergence of animals outwardly like ourselves, whose radically false beliefs were completely disconnected from their behavior. I confess I cannot make much sense of this suggestion. If our beliefs do not produce our overt actions, then what does? Are we to imagine ourselves as having two sets of beliefs, a mostly true set that governs behavior, and another, mostly false set that always hides itself from view? How would that work? And what sort of barrier would prevent the mostly false beliefs from ever making themselves known? The mostly false beliefs would need to be embedded inside very complex, highly ordered neural systems. Such systems cannot arise entirely by chance. Only selective pressures exerted over many millennia could bring them forth. But since the systems in question are supposed not to have any impact on behavior, there is no way that natural selection could do the required work. It would thus be impossible for necessary cognitive architecture ever to evolve.

Could evolution, unaided by God, produce an apparently intelligent and outwardly rational species, whose members nonetheless had radically false beliefs? To make his case Plantinga must argue, not just that there exists some bare logical possibility of this happening, but that it is rather likely to happen. Were his argument to succeed, we atheists would be hoist with our own petards. We could place no trust in the reliability of our belief-generating mechanisms, and so could have no confidence in any conclusions we might arrive at through reasoning—including, of course, the conclusion that atheism is likely to be true. With our self-esteem ruined, Plantinga could then lure us into accepting theism, on the grounds that only God could underwrite the reliability of our cognitive faculties. Yet attempts to mate radically false belief sets to outwardly normal behavior always lead to absurdity. There is no real possibility of seeing the two conjoined in the way that Plantinga demands. Plantinga's campaign to make atheism seem irrational thus falls flat.

Given an atheistic world view, there is no reason to suppose our cognitive faculties to be especially unreliable. They pretty much have to be reliable. W. V. O. Quine was right when he declared, "Creatures inveterately wrong in their inductions have a pathetic but praiseworthy tendency to die before reproducing their kind." We are all descended from ancestors who made mostly correct inductions. We have inherited their tendency toward cognitive accuracy. This tendency, furthermore, has been accumulating in our genetic line for thousands of generations through natural selection. It would appear, then, that contrary to our original premise, natural selection did "care" about truth. An aptitude for distinguishing truth from falsehood—or what

Descartes called "good sense"—was one of the traits selected for during our long evolutionary history. We may not enjoy as much good sense as we would like, but what we do have is not an accident, even if God had no part in our creation.[xxix]

Section 27

MONKEYS

I am afraid it was Darwin himself who opened the door to Plantinga's argument. In a letter to a friend, written when he was in his seventies, Darwin confessed to having entertained some doubts regarding the credentials of our cognitive systems. Plantinga quotes from that letter as follows:

> the horrid doubt always arises whether the convictions of a man's mind, which has been developed from the mind of the lower animals, are of any value or at all trustworthy. Would anyone trust in the convictions of a monkey's mind, if there are any convictions in such a mind?[xxx]

I for one have no qualms about trusting the opinions of monkeys. They have mostly true beliefs, for the same reason we do. In fact, monkeys, house cats, and other "lower animals" probably have a higher percentage of true beliefs than do the majority of humans; this is due to the fact that such animals confine their opinions to subjects familiar to them, and upon which they can be considered experts. It is only in man that we find a high proportion of false beliefs, for people are fond of forming opinions concerning matters they know nothing about, matters that have only the most distant connection to their well-being. There are benefits to this noetic prodigality of ours. Philosophy could hardly exist without it. We pay the price, however, by filling our heads with as much nonsense as wisdom.

Could Plantinga have misread Darwin's letter? Plantinga assumed that Darwin meant to express a radical skepticism about human cognition. According to such skepticism, the outward coherence of our actions entails nothing concerning the verisimilitude of our beliefs. It is thus possible that human beings are totally clueless and that we do not know which way is up, how many thumbs we have, or how to tell teddy bears from grizzly bears. Yet such skepticism, as we have seen, is absurd, and Darwin, always a sober and cautious thinker, was unlikely to have been saying anything so extreme. It may be significant that he used the term "convictions" instead of the more usual "beliefs" or "opinions." We can have beliefs or opinions about anything; convictions are generally reserved for lofty subjects. I believe that Mikey has whiskers, and that my Apple computer weighs less than twenty pounds. I do not have convictions about such things. I might, however, have convictions about the Second Amendment, or the historicity of Jesus. Monkeys do not have any convictions in this sense. Only people do.

Distinguishing convictions from ordinary beliefs leads to a different interpretation of Darwin's letter. On this reading Darwin was not doubting people's good sense when it comes to forming basic perceptual beliefs or making simple inferences, he was only expressing skepticism concerning people's deeply entrenched convictions about politics, metaphysics, ethics, and religion. There is nothing radical or subversive in this more moderate variety of skepticism. On the contrary, such skepticism is quite healthy. Basically all Darwin is saying is that when large-brained primates such as ourselves venture beyond the familiar realm of concrete daily life and start forming convictions about abstract issues, we are very likely to go wrong. The brains designed for survival on the African savanna might prove very clumsy tools for discerning truths in religion and philosophy.

Darwin was not telling us anything we did not already know. Putting evolutionary theory aside, it is evident that human beings can acquire a great deal of accurate information about the world. We know that grass is green, that sky is blue, that most of us have two thumbs, and so on. We can arrive at widespread agreement concerning such simple issues. Yet it is equally evident that people cherish a tremendous diversity of incompatible convictions concerning the aforementioned topics of politics, religion, metaphysics, and ethics. Such diversity entails that no matter what the truth might be, a large portion of mankind must be flat wrong about subjects concerning which they feel quite certain. When it comes to forming convictions on lofty issues, then, our faculties must be extremely fallible, and hence not entirely reliable.

Although evolutionary theory does not uncover any new facts regarding the trustworthiness of human cognition, it does offer a satisfying explanation for facts already well known. On many issues, evolutionary tells us, we are extremely likely to get things right, because if we entirely lacked the ability to tell the true from the false, our species would quickly die out. But while natural selection has a vested interest in ensuring that most of our ordinary beliefs should be true, it has no comparable interest in our convictions, False beliefs about metaphysics or religion will not kill us off the way false beliefs about tigers and bananas might. Biologically speaking, false convictions might even be useful to us, by making us feel better about ourselves, by cementing social bonds, or by motivating a variety of adaptive behaviors. It would thus not be very surprising if natural selection endowed us with a strong propensity to embrace a host of convenient fictions and pleasing illusions.

Darwinian naturalism thus explains both the reliable and the unreliable aspects of human cognition. Can Plantinga's theistic epistemology do likewise? I think not. Plantinga divides the design plan for human cognition into a variety of separate modules. Some of these, he says, are aimed at truth, while the rest have other objectives. A belief only counts as knowledge for Plantinga if it is generated by the proper functioning of the modules that are truth directed. Although Plantinga pays only cursory attention to the truth-obscuring modules, there would appear to be quite a few of them. The human brain seems to have modules for rationalization, excuse making, wishful thinking, ego massaging, butt covering, blame shifting, spin doctoring, euphemism generation, verbal trickery, self-deception, and outright lying, to name only a few. If natural selection designed us, then the existence of these modules makes sense. Such modules were useful; they helped our ancestors avoid the truth whenever the truth was inconvenient. But why would the Christian God include all these anti-truth modules in his design plan for the human mind? Surely God would have wanted us to be excellent philosophers and courageous confronters of the truth. Had God either created us directly, or orchestrated the evolution of our species, one cannot help thinking that the end result would have been much different, and far better. That God should have designed us in such an odd fashion is thus something of a mystery.

Section 28

TRUST

The belief that our cognitive faculties are reliable is, in one way, a belief such as any other, subject in principle to falsification or revision. As such, it meets with refutations daily. Nothing can be more obvious to us than the fallibility of our faculties. Yet we do not abandon this belief, which remains among the hardest and least brittle in our collection. This is not irrational of us—quite the contrary. Nothing could be more rational than a presumption of reliability, for without it, all thinking and believing would come to a dead stop. Abandonment of the belief would constitute intellectual suicide. The injunction that we should presume our faculties to be reliable except when we have grounds in specific cases for skepticism, belongs to that family of necessary presuppositions that lie at the heart of all rational inquiry and, indeed, of all intelligible thought. We can no more abandon this presumption than we can abandon *modus ponens*, Occam's razor, or the principle of credulity. We do not need to postulate God in order to justify our presumption of reliability. The arrows of justification run in the opposite direction, because the belief that there is a God, like belief in any other purported matter of fact, depends upon a tacit prior acceptance of the necessary presuppositions.

In his 1978 work, *Does God Exist?*, the German theologian Hans Kung offers an argument broadly similar to Plantinga's, but whereas Plantinga argued that we need God to underwrite the trust we place in our faculties, Kung claimed that God is required to make sense of our trust in reality. Kung sought to place atheists on the horns of a dilemma. Either we trust reality, without being able to say why, or we mistrust it, and so fall prey to nihilism and despair. The only solution, Kung thinks, is to postulate God as the ultimate and supremely trustworthy ground of all existence.

Someone, I do not remember who it was, once quipped that getting atheists to agree on anything was like herding cats. Atheists are just too independent-minded to gather their thoughts into a consensus. Every atheist, then, can be expected to give his or her own unique response to Kung's challenge. As for myself, I neither trust reality, nor mistrust it, at least not literally. In its proper signification, the word "trust" applies primarily to relationships between persons. I trust my family, friends, and coworkers. With greater circumspection, I also trust many strangers in certain situations: the tellers at my bank, the nurses at the emergency room, and the police officers who respond when I call 911. I mistrust most salesmen, lawyers, and politicians. But I do not in any comparable manner either trust or mistrust reality. I see no need to do either. The idea that I must do one or the other, or risk falling into nihilistic despair, strikes me as being a piece of sophistry, like that employed by McCallum when he tried to convince his readers that a godless world would be the *Worst Party Ever*.

A common tactic of sophistry is to make an opponent's position look ridiculous by restating it in one's own terms. This imposes on the opponent whatever background assumptions might be suggested or implied by said terms. When the contradiction between those background assumptions and the opponent's views is exposed, the views in question appear to be refuted. Kung's argument is sophistical in this way. By casting the debate between theism and atheism in terms of trust, he inserts into the discussion his own assumption that reality must be treated as if it was a person. Such an assumption is incompatible with atheism, for atheism holds that reality is neither a person nor governed or created by one. An atheist who agrees to Kung's terms will be trapped; he must look for a person within, behind, or above the world, toward whom trust might be directed. To escape Kung's trap, an atheist need only insist that the language of personal relationships be kept out of any attempt to paraphrase his position.

A defender of Kung might counter with an equally stubborn insistence that atheists do trust reality whether they wish to or not, provided we allow for a loose and metaphorical extension of the word "trust." This is this sense of "trust" in which a carpenter "trusts" his tools, or in which I "trust" my car to get me to work on time. But precisely because this type of trust is only metaphorical, it does not require that any real person be postulated to back it up. To say that I "trust" reality is simply to say that I expect certain component parts of reality, such as automobiles and rotary saws, to behave in a more or less predictable manner.

Is my expectation of such predictability irrational or groundless? Certainly not. Among the necessary presuppositions of rationality is an axiom to the effect that we ought to prefer simple world views to more complex ones. Now, of course, we cannot know *a priori* that the world is going to be simple, any more than we can know that appearances will never be deceiving, or that the number of entities will be conveniently limited. Still, just as our methodological rules call upon us to apply Occam's razor and the credulity principle, so those same rules urge us to follow the KISS principle in all of our theorizing: "Keep it super simple." Yet in the relevant sense of "simple," a world that operates according to laws is simpler than one that does not, and a world that obeys one set of laws throughout its history is simpler than one wherein the laws change frequently or at random. We should, then, interpret the phenomena according to the simplest scheme of laws that will fit. This interpretive rule underlies all of our inductions and all of our empirical, inferential, and probabilistic reasoning. That, together with our daily experience of nature's regular and predictable operation, is what justifies my expectation that the future will be similarly regular and predictable.

To be fair, Kung was not suggesting that we postulate God in order to justify our confidence in induction. Kung was concerned instead with the value, meaning, and purpose of human life. He thought that without God, we would have no reason to think that human life had any meaning, value, or purpose. Whatever confidence we might profess to have in the significance of our lives must, in the absence of God, float unsupported. But Kung's worries need not trouble any atheist. For an atheist, human life has value because *we* value it; it has meaning because it means something to *us*. Purposes are not assigned to us by any external source; instead, they are what we choose for ourselves. So we need not trust reality to provide us with meaning, value, or purpose. Things actually work the other way around. Whatever value, meaning, or purpose the universe possesses, it possesses in virtue of the fact that it contains sentient, rational beings such as ourselves. The universe, you might say, only created life, rationality, and sentience. It is up to sentient, rational life to decide for itself what makes life, sentience, and rationality worthwhile.

Section 29

BLINTZES

The elders of Chelm faced a crisis. The townsfolk could not properly celebrate an upcoming holiday without serving blintzes. To make blintzes, they needed sour cream, yet none was available. What to do? The elders thought long and hard, until one of them discovered a solution: they would pass a law declaring that henceforth the term "sour cream" would refer to water, and "water" to sour cream. This would ensure a plentiful supply of sour cream for the holiday. Of course it would also produce a water shortage, but that issue could be dealt with another time.

I have retold this little parable based on Steven Pinker's account in *The Stuff of Thought*. Pinker borrowed the tale from Isaac Bashevis Singer, whose children's story *The Elders of Chelm and Genendel's Key* drew its inspiration from Yiddish folklore. For Pinker, a linguist, the moral of the story is that while language is a marvelous tool for describing reality, it neither creates the reality in which we live, nor distorts our view of it. Language does not shape thought, but thought language. Since our cognitive faculties can access reality quite independently of the words used to describe it, no one would be fooled by the kind of verbal trickery engaged in by Chelm's elders.[xxxi]

Pinker is right: no veil of language necessarily blocks our perception or reality. Yet philosophers, lawyers, politicians, and salesmen are constantly trying to manufacture such veils. Usually the attempt trips our hogwash sensors. After detecting the sophistry, we mentally tear up these flimsy veils and throw them out. Sometimes, however, the trickery works. The trickster's audience, being overeager to believe what the trickster has to say, falls into his trap. The trickster may even deceive himself; but such self-deception only makes him a better and more convincing con artist. This bewitchment of thought by means of language can and does occur, despite Pinker's attempt to deny it.

The elders' sophistical maneuver involves the stipulative redefinition of words. A stipulative redefinition does not attempt to capture a usage already in place; instead it aims to create a new meaning for some already existing term. Although the intent behind a stimulative redefinition may sometimes be benign, it can also, as we have seen, be part of a trick.

I bring this up because much of Plantinga's famous defense of Christian belief rests on stipulative redefinitions. Plantinga routinely assigns meanings to philosophical terms quite other than what they have in most philosophical discourse. He then insists that all objections to Christian belief be recast using the words and word meanings he provides. Since the recasting process renders those objections incomprehensible, Plantinga triumphantly concludes that no serious objections to Christian belief exist. Such maneuvers will fool no one except Plantinga himself, together with those overeager to accept his thesis.

Near the beginning of *Warranted Christian Belief*, Plantinga distinguishes *de facto* from *de jure* questions. Although the distinction is a useful one, Plantinga mischaracterizes it. The distinction enters philosophy from the field of law. In a murder case, the principal *de facto* question might be: "Did the defendant, Mr. N, shoot and kill the deceased?" If that question is answered in the affirmative, a *de jure* question then arises: "Did Mr. N commit murder?" The *de jure* question has to do with a point of law. It asks if the law has been broken, and whether Mr.

N's violent action was legally justified. That action would be justified if, for example, Mr. N had acted in self-defense, or while defending the life of some other innocent party. To exonerate his client, N's attorney need not show that N did the right thing, or that N chose the best course of action from among those available to him. The attorney need only argue that N adhered to the law and that his behavior met the minimum legal requirements to avoid prison.

The society of philosophers, or what Hume called the republic of letters, has no positive law. Philosophers need not fear that they will be arrested by the wisdom police and imprisoned for crimes of reflection. Yet *de jure* questions do arise in philosophy. Philosophers recognize certain normative standards of rationality. We generally make some effort to adhere to these, and we expect that our peers will honor them as well. These standards constitute the "law" to which philosophically oriented *de jure* questions refer. However, precisely because the threat of prison has been removed, there are no minimum requirements that a philosopher must meet in order to avoid prosecution. The "laws" of rationality are not about minimums but about maximums; they establish ideals of rationality to which philosophers are supposed to aspire. A *de jure* question in philosophy is thus never about what is legally tolerable or acceptable; rather, it is about what is right or best.

Now consider how this applies to Plantinga's Christian religion. If we ask: "Does the God of Christianity exist?", that is a *de facto* question, and a problem in metaphysics. The related *de jure* question would be, "Ought we to believe in that God? Is Christianity the best justified and most rational position for us to take, and is the embracing of Christian theism the best way to exemplify the epistemic values and intellectual virtues we deem to be important?" So phrased, the *de jure* question concerns a problem in the field of intellectual ethics. It presents us with an ethical challenge. To provide a proper response, a Christian has to explain what makes Christianity superior to its rivals. He needs to argue, not just that Christian doctrine represents a defensible dwelling, perhaps one among many others, or that it appeals more than the others do to his passional nature and personal preferences, but that it is, in some much more objective fashion the nicest house in the neighborhood. The Christian cannot simply pit faith against faith, or faith against lack of faith. He must instead appeal to reason, just as Locke maintained in the *Essay Concerning Human Understanding.* A failure to heed Locke's insight in this matter will make the Christian's loyalty to his faith seem arbitrary.

Ought we to believe in God, or in any being like the one described in traditional Christian doctrines? Instead of answering this question, Plantinga does everything he can to avoid it. Plantinga is not so much interested in *de jure* questions about his faith as he is in *de jure* objections to it. With his focus on traditional objections to Christianity, Plantinga adopts the stance of Christianity's defense attorney. He argues not that Christianity is right but rather that its critics have not yet succeeded in proving that there is anything wrong with it. But achieving even this seemingly modest objective requires Chelmian sophistry.

Plantinga's preferred formulation of the *de jure* question is to ask whether Christian theism is warranted. The corresponding objection would then consist in the claim that Christian theism is not warranted. Plantinga calls this the F & M complaint, "F & M" being short for "Freud and Marx." The designation is grossly unfair to both authors. Neither Freud nor Marx phrased their opposition to theism in terms of warrant. Had they used that word, they would not have meant it the way Plantinga does. Neither man would appreciate Plantinga's attempt to force them to speak his language.

Formulation of the *de jure* question in terms of warrant is open to two objections. First, it assumes that we are willing to accept the account of warrant that Plantinga offered in his earlier work, *Warrant and Proper Function.* I have already given multiple reasons for rejecting that account. Second, the question "Is Christian theism warranted?" is not a genuine *de jure* question. A *de jure* question necessarily concerns some point of law, be it positive law, moral law, or some logical or epistemological "law." Warrant, as Plantinga conceives of it, has nothing to do with law. Achieving Plantingian warrant is a matter not of obeying laws but of operating according to a design plan. If we ask whether something is functioning properly, given its design, that is not a legal question but an engineering issue. I am all in favor of addressing engineering issues, but I must object when a *de facto* question of engineering masquerades as any kind of *de jure* question. Plantinga's effort to substitute a *de facto* for a *de jure* question is clearly illicit.

Plantinga argues that an objection to Christian theism based on warrant must inevitably fail. On this point he is absolutely right. According to Plantinga, a belief is warranted "if it is produced by cognitive processes or faculties that are functioning properly, in a cognitive environment that is propitious for that exercise of cognitive powers, according to a design plan that is successfully aimed at the production of true belief." But if Christian theism were true, then our cognitive environment would be propitious for such theism, and Christians, in arriving at their beliefs, would presumably be functioning just as God intended them to. It follows that if Christianity were true, then acceptance of it would be entirely warranted, at least in Plantinga's sense of the term. To claim that Christianity is not warranted in that sense, one must assume that it is false. Since the falsehood of Christianity is supposed to belong to the objector's conclusion, not to his premise, a warrant-based objection to Christianity cannot get off the ground. This, however, is an entirely uninteresting and trivial result. Perhaps Christianity would enjoy Plantingian warrant if it was true. Judaism would also be warranted if it was true, and so too would Islam, Buddhism, Hinduism, and, of course, atheism. So all Plantinga has really proven is that his own concept of warrant is absolutely useless when considered as a guide to assessing the relative merits of different religious outlooks. Few atheists will find this result disturbing.

Plantinga also considers an objection to Christianity based on rationality, The objection would be that Christian beliefs are irrational. Plantinga claims to find considerable difficulty in understanding the concept of rationality that underpins this particular objection. Now mind you, he has no trouble at all with the concept of rationality when he is critiquing the views of other thinkers. His sometimes scathing criticisms of Kant, Freud, Marx, Nietzsche, and many others suggest that he thinks he knows perfectly well what rationality is, and how to tell rational positions from irrational ones. But when Christian doctrines are called into question, suddenly the concept of rationality seems opaque to him. His solution is to conceive of rationality in terms of warrant. If a belief is warranted, then it is also rational, for rationality, like warrant, is a matter of the proper function of truth-directed faculties according to a given design plan.

Plantinga's view of rationality has the consequence that we cannot know whether one of our beliefs is rational unless we know which module within our minds produced it, and what that module is designed to do. The further consequence is that we cannot know whether Christian theism is rational unless we understand the design plan of the human mind, and this in turn requires that we know whether or not there is a God. If no God exists, then perhaps theism is, as Freud said, a product of wishful thinking. In that case, all forms of theism may very well be irrational. On the other hand, if God does exist, then he would have designed the human mind so that it would be naturally inclined to believe in him. Whatever mechanisms lead to belief in God must therefore be truth-directed, and part of a design plan "successfully aimed at the production of true belief." That would make Christianity rational, according to Plantinga's conception of rationality. It also means that no objection to Christianity based on that conception can hope to succeed, since, once again, the objection would have to assume that Christianity is false, which is the very point in dispute.

This conclusion is just as uninteresting and trivial as the one before. No real atheist would found his objections to Christianity on Plantinga's concept of rationality. That concept has only a distant connection to our ordinary, common sense understanding of what rationality is. We normally think that we can tell whether a belief is rational without inquiring into what module produced it, or how that module fits into a design plan, or whether the module was malfunctioning. Rationality, as we normally conceive of it, has nothing to do with any of that. So whether Christianity is rational according to Plantinga's made-up notion of it is of no importance to us.

What about an objection to Christianity based on justification? Are Christian doctrines justified? Plantinga thinks it quite obvious that they are, and that Christians are plenty justified in accepting them. However, in the same passage where he asserts this, he concedes that, given his conception of justification, the beliefs of lunatics residing in insane asylums are also justified. But here one must wonder: If "justified" does not entail "sane," then has the concept of justification not been watered down? And how, precisely, does this tacit redefinition of justification differ from the attempt by the elders of Chelm to water down the concept of sour cream?[xxxii]

Section 30

CONTRADICTIONS

Faith, I claim, is bad for the brain. Whether adopted as the result of a wager, or through the promptings of one's passional nature, or as the conclusion of sophistical arguments, faith has the power to corrupt otherwise excellent minds. A perfect example of this comes from the writings of the theologian Richard Swinburne, who ties his brain up in knots trying to reconcile the text of the Bible with his faith that the Bible is God's Word.

If God in some sense wrote the Bible, then of course every sentence in it must be both true and in accord with every other sentence. This does not at first glance appear to be the case. The Bible frequently seems to contradict itself and to clash with well-established scientific facts. In *Revelation: From Metaphor to Analogy*, Swinburne explains the techniques for making these contradictions go away. Consider how he handles the apparent disagreement between the conception of Christ that Paul offers in Romans, and that presented by John:

> Paul, a servant of Christ Jesus, called to be an apostle and set apart for the gospel of God— the gospel he promised beforehand through his prophets in the Holy Scriptures regarding his Son, who as to his earthly life was a descendant

of David, and who through the Spirit of holiness was appointed the Son of God in power by his resurrection from the dead: Jesus Christ our Lord. Through him we received grace and apostleship to call all the Gentiles to faith and obedience for his name's sake. And you also are among those Gentiles who are called to belong to Jesus Christ (Romans 1:1–6, Today's New International Version).

In the beginning was the Word, and the Word was with God, and the Word was God. He was with God in the beginning. Through him all things were made; without him nothing was made … The true light that gives light to everyone was coming into the world. He was in the world, and though the world was made through him, the world did not recognize him. He came to that which was his own, but his own did not receive him. Yet to all who did receive him, to those who believed in his name, he gave the right to become children of God— children born not of natural descent, nor of human decision or a husband's will, but born of God. The Word became flesh and made his dwelling among us. We have seen his glory, the glory of the one and only Son, who came from the Father, full of grace and truth (John 1:1–14, omitting lines 4–8, Today's New International Version).

These two passages will not trouble an atheist—or a Jew or Muslim either. Paul and John simply disagree. Paul's Jesus became the Son of God at the end of his earthly existence; John's Jesus entered into his earthly existence as the Son, having always enjoyed that status. John wrote several decades after Paul. It should surprise no one that Jesus should have grown in stature during the intervening years. One can imagine rival factions of early Christians competing with one another for converts. Each faction might seek to outdo the others by claiming to worship a greater, loftier, and nobler Jesus. There would then be a kind of "arms race" pressuring the rival factions to equip themselves with ever mightier objects of worship. This process would eventually reach its logical limit, at which point Jesus would be equated with God. John represents that logical limit, and it was his view of Jesus that became official church doctrine. Paul might not have approved, but once he and his contemporaries got the ball rolling, there was nothing any of them could have done to stop the process.

Swinburne takes the orthodox view and sides with John. However, that same orthodoxy commits him to accepting Romans as divine revelation. What Romans says about Jesus must therefore be correct. But if John is correct, then Romans cannot be correct. To escape this dilemma, Swinburne has to find a way to disagree with Paul, while still agreeing with what God says through Paul.

Swinburne concedes that Paul believed what he appears to have believed about Jesus. By Swinburne's logic, it follows that the first chapter of Romans cannot really mean what it appears to mean. The same logic suggests that Paul could not have known what his text really meant; nor should we, the modern readers of Paul, confuse its meaning with the beliefs its human author wished to express. To do that, Swinburne says, is to commit the "genetic fallacy." If we want to know what the quoted passage from Romans really means, we need to place it in its proper context. For Swinburne, this context includes the rest of the New Testament, together with church doctrines that were not formulated until centuries later. Those doctrines make John's position the correct one, and this "forces" (Swinburne's term) a reinterpretation of Paul.

The reinterpretation focuses on the Greek word "oristhentos," which the New International Version translates as "appointed," but that could also be translated as "made." Although "appointed" and "made" are both very natural ways to bring the Greek into modern English, they suffer the defect of putting Paul's theology at odds with the Catholic faith. Consequently, says Swinburne, we must take "oristhentos" to mean "recognized as." The Holy Spirit did not make Jesus the Son of God; it merely recognized in him a status he already possessed. Swinburne admits that this is a very unnatural way to render the Greek, but since it is the only way to reconcile Paul with John, it must be correct.

Yet it cannot be correct. Swinburne's analysis misfires on several fronts. For one thing, he clearly misapplies the term "genetic fallacy." It is no fallacy to link the meaning of a text to the ideas its author was trying to communicate. If that were a fallacy, then Swinburne would be guilty of it too. Swinburne surely wants to tie the meaning of Romans to an author's intentions. The only difference between him and non-Christian readers is that non-Christians will take the author to be Paul alone, while Swinburne assumes that behind Paul stands the real author, namely God.

Swinburne's comments about Paul's context are equally misguided. Everyone agrees that an author's words should be taken in context. Yet this universal agreement among sensible readers only applies to what we might call the natural context of a passage. For Romans 1:1–6, the natural context would presumably include such things as: the rest of Romans; Paul's other writings; the linguistic and cultural conventions in effect when he wrote; plus the historical events that shaped both Paul's consciousness and that of his first century audience. Church creeds can hardly belong to Paul's natural context, since they were not formulated until long after Paul died. Calling John part of Paul's context makes no sense either. Paul never so much as heard of John, who may not even have been born yet when Paul wrote. Nothing links Paul's writings to those of John except a decision made by the Catholic Church in the fourth century to put both men's works in the New Testament. How can that arbitrary and very late decision possibly change the meaning of Paul's words?

Swinburne, though, insists that it did change the meaning. In putting together the modern Bible, Swinburne claims, the Catholic Church created a new document, and with it, a new context of interpretation. This action liberated Romans from Paul's intentions, and authorized future theologians to see Romans as God's vehicle for revealing divine meanings of which Paul could have had no inkling.

The motivation for forcing this twisted interpretation onto Paul's text is to rescue God's dignity as an author. No Catholic theologian can allow God to contradict himself; whatever God says through Paul must therefore be brought into line with what he says through John. Unfortunately Swinburne's rescue attempt fails miserably. God still comes out looking verbally inept. No competent speaker who believed what John believed about Jesus would say what Paul says at the beginning of Romans. Swinburne's translation of "oristhentos" is not just awkward and unnatural—it turns what is supposed to be high drama into something comical. Romans 1:1–6 strongly suggests that "recognition" by the Holy Spirit was a major, even transformative event. If it were not, there would be no point to mentioning it during so brief a summary of Jesus's life. But if John was right about Jesus's true nature, then Jesus did not need the Holy Spirit to "recognize" him, nor could acquiring such recognition have constituted, as Paul's text insists it does, an important part of the Resurrection's purpose. Certainly the Resurrection would not have provided the Holy Spirit with any new information. Hadn't the Holy Spirit already been briefed on who Jesus was? If we force John's Christology onto Romans, the "recognition" mentioned becomes an utterly trivial episode. For one member of the Trinity to suddenly "recognize" another seems actually to be absurd. It would be just as if one were to return home after a short trip to hear one's wife of twenty years exclaim, "I recognize you; you're my husband!" It is no wonder that John fails to mention the "recognition." It seems utterly unintelligible that God should bother to mention it through Paul.

I do not criticize Swinburne because I think the job of reconciling Paul with John could have been done better, but because in my view the job should not be done at all. Any interpretation of Paul that forces him into agreement with John will necessarily employ either willful mistranslations of ancient words or other sophistries equally blatant. There is just no way to make God the author of both texts without both disrespecting the texts and impugning God's writing skills.

This is not an isolated case. The Bible contains a thousand other contradictions, none of which can be erased except through painfully convoluted reasoning. Taken all together, these conflicting passages constitute an overwhelming cumulative argument for rejecting the belief that the Bible had a divine author. Were a single omniscient mind behind the Bible, it could and would have guided its human scribes toward a far more coherent result. Since that obviously did not happen, the thesis of divine authorship should be regarded not merely as implausible, but as falsified.

Unfortunately, Swinburne's faith forbids him to see anything in the Bible as evidence against his belief that God wrote it. All of his techniques of biblical interpretation are carefully designed to deny even the possibility of there being contrary evidence when it comes to church doctrine. His faith thus promotes a kind of macular degeneration of the intellect, blinding him to what is plainly visible. Inevitably it also promotes hypocrisy. Swinburne gladly makes use of evidence whenever he thinks it speaks for his beliefs, and he fully expects his readers to receive his purported evidence with an open mind. Yet faith prevents him from returning the favor, for when the evidence speaks against his beliefs, he simply cannot consider the idea that those beliefs might be false. This evidence-denying function of faith corrupts the mind; the stronger the faith, the more thorough the corruption. There can be no better argument against faith than that.

Section 31

GENESIS

Gerald Schroeder is an MIT-trained physicist and amateur theologian. In his 1990 work, *Genesis and the Big Bang*, Schroeder attempts to reconcile his reading of the Bible with his knowledge of contemporary physics. He argues that modern cosmology does not refute, but actually corroborates, the Word of God.

Genesis does anticipate modern cosmology on some points. For example, both hold that the world has not existed forever. Genesis says that God created the heavens and the earth "in the beginning"; science confirms that the universe began with a massive explosion known as "the big bang." Such parallels should not surprise us. The writings of ancient and medieval authors are full of them. Democritus, after all, foresaw modern atomic theory; Anaximander shrewdly guessed that terrestrial animals must have emerged from the sea. The medieval Jewish sage Nahmanides came eerily close to big bang theory when he speculated that the universe originated from a primordial mass no larger than a mustard seed.

No one can dispute that there is important wisdom in old books. It is only when Schroeder and others insist on finding superhuman wisdom there that troubles arise. For what Schroeder aims to demonstrate is not merely the occasional accord between Genesis and modern science, but a perfect and unerring harmony.

The conceptual contortions his project requires are truly staggering, and coming from the otherwise brilliant mind of a nuclear physicist, rather tragic.

The cover of *The Ladder* depicted a prehistoric cave painting from Altamira, Spain. The painting, which is at least thirteen thousand years old, was discovered in 1879. Many experts initially doubted its authenticity. They did not believe Paleolithic people could create such exquisite art. Their skepticism was overcome when it became clear that there were many other beautifully decorated caves around Europe. These paintings give us the overwhelming impression of having been done by real human artists, people endowed with the same mental and spiritual faculties we enjoy today. They cannot be the product of instinct, the way beehives and beaver damns are. Appearing as they do deep inside their caves, the paintings demanded that their artists paint what they could not immediately see. The paintings do not necessarily depict animals from any particular hunt; instead, they appear to be representations of the kinds of animals with which the artists were familiar. This would have involved a very human level of both imagination and conceptualization. Such painting must have taken many hours to complete. yet they served no obvious practical purpose. Perhaps they had religious significance; perhaps they indicate attempts to magically influence the outcome of future hunts. Perhaps they were simply forms of self-expression. But animals do not have religion, or believe in magic. No mere animal would go to so much trouble just for fun. Only people do these things.

The archeological record confirms what the paintings tell us. Thirteen thousand years ago, people essentially like us walked the earth. They manufactured sophisticated stone tools, wore stitched clothing, hunted with bows and arrows, and fashioned jewelry. They engaged in trade, had complex social structures, and, as Schroeder admits, they almost certainly spoke human languages. In short, they lived very much like the fully human hunter-gatherer groups who survived well into modern times.

Schroeder is not convinced. He "knows" that the Bible is the Word of God. The Bible tells him that Adam, the first true man, lived about six thousand years ago. Therefore no one living before then could have had a soul; they must all have been soulless automatons. The appearance of humanity produced by their paintings and other archeological remains therefore has to be just an illusion.

If we met in person with beings who had human bodies, and spoke with them, and saw them wearing neatly sewn pants and shirts that they had made themselves, and then dined with them on beef roasted over their own fire, it would be a sign of severe mental illness to deny that they were real people. Yet Schroeder's faith puts a halo of sanctity around just such craziness.

Schroeder's thinking resembles that done by young earth creationists who maintain that the earth is less than ten thousand years old, and who dismiss all evidence to the contrary as so much illusion. However, since he is a professional physicist, Schroeder cannot abandon his belief that the earth was formed more than four billion years ago, and that the universe began with a bang several billion years before that. Neither, of course, can he reject the Bible's testimony that God created the heavens and the earth in six days. How can Schroeder keep both his science and his faith?

Invoking Einstein's concept of time dilation, Schroeder asserts that in God's frame of reference, just six literal twenty-four-hour days passed between the big bang and the breathing of life into Adam. The two events are separated by billions of years only in our earthly referential frame. So you see, it is all a matter of perspective.

Schroeder's solution is wildly implausible. The transcendent God of Judeo-Christian tradition is not in space and time, so he cannot have a frame of reference in the sense required by Einstein's theories. We can, if we like, speak of there being a God's-eye point of view, but since God is thought to be immanent within his creation, his point of view incorporates every other. He lurks simultaneously within every referential frame.

According to Einstein, time dilation is caused by motion and gravity. The clocks of any two observers will tick at different speeds if they are moving relative to another, or if they operate within gravitational fields of different strengths. The faster you move, and the stronger your gravitational field, the slower your clock will tick relative to the clocks of other observers. But God does not move, nor is he subject to gravity—on the contrary, gravity is subject to him. There is thus no way for his clock ever to get out of sync with earthly clocks. That is assuming God even has a clock.

Schroeder, however, needs God to have exactly one divine clock, and he needs that clock to speed up and slow down in the most chaotic manner. The first "day" in Genesis might have been, from our point of view, only a few thousand years long. Schroeder says it took about that much time for the universe's earliest photons to separate from ordinary matter: "Let there be light." Obviously, though, days two through five must have consumed hundreds of millions, if not billions, of years each. Then, Schroeder tells us, God's clock magically falls into sync with earthly clocks with the creation of Adam on the sixth day. How convenient!

Genesis 1:2 describes the "wind" or spirit of God hovering over the waters. One might naively suppose that this was just a poetic way of emphasizing God's immediate presence during Creation. Schroeder thinks it is much more than that. He claims that the "wind" is actually an obscure force that physicists introduce into their equations to explain why the universe inflated during its earliest moments. Genesis does not attribute this or any other function to the wind. "Hovering" is not "inflating." Getting from the one to the other demands a Swinburnian degree of willful mistranslation. The sole connection between the wind and the force is that both are unique phenomena. Genesis only mentions the wind once; physicists only invoke the force once. The force sounds rather *ad hoc*. Perhaps scientists will eventually learn how to do without it. Yet Schroeder believes that thirty-four hundred years ago on Mount Sinai, God inserted into Genesis a secret reference to this special force, knowing that science would eventually uncover the passage's true meaning.

God's interest in such minute technical details seems to evaporate quickly. Genesis 1:11 has God creating fruit trees on day three. The sun, the moon, and the stars do not appear until day four. This reverses the correct order; those celestial bodies antedate fruit trees by billions of years. Schroeder has a twofold strategy for handling this. First, he makes "fruit trees" refer to the earliest plant life, namely blue-green algae. Second, he assumes that what the fourth day of Genesis describes is not the creation of the celestial bodies, but instead their first appearance to observers on earth. The earth's atmosphere up until then was apparently very soupy; it was not until after algae emerged that the atmosphere thinned out enough to allow earth-bound observers to see the heavens.

Schroeder's account is incoherent. His theory of the divine time dilation required Genesis's account of days three and four be written from God's point of view. His fruit trees theory, though, requires that those same passages be written from the perspective of purely hypothetical earthly observers. Schroeder takes no notice of this contradiction.

Genesis 1:1 clearly states that "In the beginning, God created the heavens and the earth." The author of Genesis thus adopts as one of his primary themes God's creation of the heavens. But if Schroeder is right, then Genesis never actually describes the heavens' creation; it only announces when the heavens became visible, a seemingly inconsequential event, since there were no people around to see the heavens until much later. The creation of literal trees is also passed by in silence, even though most of Genesis's audience would probably be more interested in trees than in pond scum.

If, as Schroeder believes, God wrote Genesis, then God's decisions concerning what to mention and what to leave out seem very bizarre. God's manner of shifting perspectives without notice, and for no apparent reason, is equally queer. You would think God might be a better writer. But like Swinburne, Schroeder is oblivious to this relentless denigration of God's expository talents.

Although Schroeder sought to unite faith with reason, he managed to preserve the one only by corrupting the other. He essentially used Genesis as a glorified ink blot, reading his own cosmological beliefs into it. He thereby turned a beautifully expressed myth into a garbled rendition of twentieth century ideas. Modern physics does not fit onto the Bible's Procrustean bed. Attempts to make it fit are an insult to our intelligence. How sad that faith prevents Schroeder from seeing that.

Section 32

THE FALLACY

Swinburne and Schroeder both commit what I call the disciple's fallacy. This fallacy consists in adopting an *a priori* faith in the unerring validity of some text, and thenceforth displaying a dogmatic willingness to use any sophistry necessary to maintain that pretense of perfection. Victims of the fallacy apply a double standard: other books are true when proven true, while their sacred text must be true, come what may. The perversity of the fallacy may be seen in this, that the more forced and artificial interpretations of the sacred text become, the more convinced the fallacy's victims are that their sacred text contains infinite depths of meaning, which they are busy bringing to light. The victims do not see apparent errors in the text as any disconfirmation of their beliefs. Such "errors," in their view, merely present challenges of interpretation. The greater the challenge, the stronger their faith grows when the challenge is met. Often the sacred text in question does express profound wisdom; that, however, cannot justify the use of twisted logic to get at it.

THE CASE FOR ATHEISM

Section 1

THE LANGURS

The initial two-thirds of Kenneth Miller's *Finding Darwin's God* are a masterpiece of scientific reasoning. Miller defends modern Darwinism and skewers the creationists, whose weak arguments for their religious preconceptions get fully exposed for what they are. Darwin's theory of evolution by natural selection, Miller argues, has been confirmed time and again, both in the field and in the lab. The evidence for it could not be stronger. Sadly, in the final third of his book, Miller begins to do exactly what he caught the creationists doing: he abandons reason in favor of rationalization. His evidentialism goes out the window as he tries vainly to reconcile his faith with the facts.

A hint of what is to come appears in Miller's first chapter, entitled "Darwin's Apple." Miller quotes a passage from *The Pony Fish's Glow*, written by fellow evolutionist George C. Williams:

> She [anthropologist Sarah Hrdy] studied a population of monkeys, Hanuman langurs, in Northern India. Their mating system is what biologists call harem polygyny: dominant males have exclusive sexual access to a group of adult females, as long as they can keep other males away. Sooner or later, a stronger male usurps the

> harem and the defeated one must join the ranks
> of celibate outcastes. The new male shows his
> love for his new wives by trying to kill their
> unweaned infants. For each successful killing, a
> mother stops lactating and goes into estrous ...
> Deprived of her nursing baby, a female soon
> starts ovulating. She accepts the advances of
> her baby's murderer, and he becomes the father
> of her next child.
>
> Do you still think God is good?[xxxiii]

The langur case is well chosen. Primates like ourselves, langurs are similar enough to humans to elicit our sympathy. Langurs can feel pain; they can suffer. The life of a langur has value. No one cares if you squash a bee. If you mistreat a langur, you deserve to be arrested for animal abuse. Williams succinctly recounts how the langurs regularly abuse their own kind. Their social system seems designed to produce gratuitous suffering for the mothers, infants and defeated males who are the victims of that abuse. Yet langurs are not intelligent enough to be considered moral agents. We cannot blame *them* for what they do. If anyone were to blame, it would be God, who is ultimately responsible for what he has created. It makes no difference that the langurs came into existence through an evolutionary process rather than through a direct act of divine creation. God, if there is one, chose to use evolution as the means of his handiwork. What it does, he does. If evolution seems mindless, indifferent, and completely amoral, then this reflects very badly on God.

Miller wants to affirm that God is good. Apparently there is nothing that he would accept as evidence to the contrary. Describing Williams's remarks as taking "withering potshots at God," Miller defends his deity by insisting that Williams "fundamentally misunderstands what faith in God implies about the nature of good and evil." He insists that the monkeys have nothing to do with God:

> To begin with, the harem-murders of Hrdy's monkeys are not moral lessons, but animal behaviors. Evolution, under some circumstances, may indeed favor the development of behaviors in which one individual kills others of its own species. For example, the first, instinctive action of a newly emerged queen bee is to sting to death her pupating sisters before they can emerge to challenge her rule. A true naturalist like Williams should recognize that any pronouncement of such behaviors as good or bad does not come from science. We find the murder of a nursing monkey shocking not in itself, and certainly not in its evolutionary logic, but only by analogy, because it is so easy to compare such actions to our own.[xxxiv]

I do not know why Miller brought up the bees. If evolutionary mechanisms do to sentient creatures such as langurs exactly what they do to unfeeling bees, that does not solve the problem at hand—it is the problem.

Miller's other comments are no more to the point. Of course, any pronouncements of the monkeys' behavior as good or bad do not come from science. Williams is speaking not just as a scientist but as a human being. Miller does likewise throughout his book. Langurs, as I am sure Williams would be willing to concede, do not really commit "murder." What they do is merely analogous to the murders committed by humans against other humans. But there is nothing "merely analogous" about any pain the langurs might experience. That is real pain, essentially no different from our own. So why wouldn't a compassionate God design the langurs' social system in a more rational manner? And why would he not design the instincts and brains of the male langurs so as to dampen their tendency toward violence?

Miller seeks to avoid Williams's "moral lesson" by drawing upon an analogy from the game of billiards. A billiards player displays more skill, Miller tells us, if he sinks all the balls with one shot, rather than using a separate shot for each ball. So too, God shows greater skill by having evolution produce species than he would if he did all the work himself, one species at a time.[xxxv]

Miller's analogy would work only if evolution could endow species with the same level of engineering perfection that God could. Unfortunately this is very far from being the case. The natural world is full of engineering imperfections caused by natural selection's lack of intelligence. The langurs are just one example of this; there are a thousand others. Miller, however, chooses to turn a blind eye to these gaffes. His God has no interest in either avoiding or rectifying them. "God," Miller declares, "decided that the living world would be physically independent of direct divine intervention." So on Miller's view, God couldn't do anything to help the langurs because that would mean violating this principle regarding the cosmos's independence. This leaves us with a God who cares more for some utterly vacuous principle than he does for his creatures' welfare, and a God who shows off with trick shots because crafting species piecemeal would be too much trouble. I cannot imagine a clearer definition of what it would mean for God to be amoral and indifferent. Yet Miller cannot see this. His faith prevents it.

Section 2

ALZHEIMER'S

When my father passed away a few years ago, the family held a small funeral service at his church. Per his instructions, his remains had been cremated, and were being interred on church grounds, along with those of my mother. My older brother, Chris, began the service. I do not remember most of what he said, only that his words were on the whole very tasteful and appropriate. Yet one of his comments grated on my nerves. I am sure it grated on mine alone. The rest of the family, which includes both Jews and Christians, no doubt considered his remark to be the epitome of heartwarming piety. Referring to our father's long struggle with Alzheimer's, Chris suggested that the disease was God's way of getting Dad to "focus on what is really important in life." I said nothing at the time; I kept my reservations to myself. Still, this attempt to whitewash God's behavior disgusted me.

My father, Robert, and I did not see eye to eye on very many things. Nonetheless, everyone who knew him would agree that he was a good man, a good husband and father, and one of the brighter tools in the shed. He did not seem to have any difficulty keeping his priorities in order. Yet according to my brother, an omniscient God determined that Robert's priorities had somehow gotten askew. God, therefore, in his infinite wisdom, decided to correct this problem by afflicting Robert with Alzheimer's. He gradually addled Robert's brains until the poor man could not carry on a conversation, recognize family members, or remember what he ate for dinner five minutes ago. All this was done to Robert *on purpose*, to teach him a lesson.

A God who "teaches" in this manner is neither wise nor good but simply a fiend. No sane deity would do what my brother believes God did, nor would he do it for the reason my brother gives. Surely, with all the resources at his disposal, God could find other, more humane ways to instruct his creatures?

Chris, a born-again Christian, is perfectly sane. He knows right from wrong as well as I do, perhaps better. Why then can he suppose God to perform horrible acts without feeling my moral revulsion? His faith apparently forbids him to apply any moral standards to God. "God is good" seems to be faith's Rule Number One. Rule Number Two holds that when God acts despicably, the faithful should just refer back to Rule Number One. These two rules not only guide my brother's thinking about God; they have dominated the minds of countless other theists throughout the centuries.

When theists describe their God in the abstract, they in their adoration heap upon him terms of the greatest imaginable praise. He is said to be omnipotent, omniscient, supremely wise, and infinitely just and merciful, not to mention the very archetype of love. He sounds wonderful, doesn't he? We cannot help wishing that such an admirable being existed. How dramatically things change when theists describe, and try to explain, the concrete actions of their God. Their accounts almost always make God sound like a monster.

There is a sense in which Jews, Christians, and Muslims have two Gods. One dwells in the abstract descriptions, the other in concrete acts. Between these two Gods lies a tremendous chasm. The abstract God represents a triumph of the human imagination. But it is the concrete God to whom the faithful actually pray, and that God is unworthy of mankind's worship.

Theists will tell me that I am being ridiculous. God, they might say, has the right to do with us as he pleases. Who are we to criticize him? C. S. Lewis captured this sentiment perfectly:

> there is a difficulty about disagreeing with God. He is the source from which all your reasoning power comes: you could not be right and he wrong any more than a stream can rise higher than its own source.[xxxvi]

But why would a genuinely good God want me to turn off my critical faculties whenever I think about him? That makes no sense. I could not do it, even if it did. I find myself impelled to think that infinite power would confer not just infinite rights, but also infinite fiduciary responsibilities. A God powerful enough to create universes and judge sinners would have an obligation to show his creatures more consideration, be they langurs or humans. Infinite power can neither justify nor excuse monstrous behavior. An omnipotent monster is still a monster.

Section 3

OPPORTUNITIES

My brother's approach to the problem of evil finds a more formal expression in Swinburne's opportunity theory. Opportunity theory is essentially the disciple's fallacy applied to the book of nature. Natural ills, like biblical contradictions, are explained away until nothing remains. Swinburne would say, for example, that Alzheimer's was Robert Marker's opportunity to realign his priorities. Perhaps it was also an opportunity for Robert's children and caregivers to practice such virtues as compassion, understanding, and self-sacrifice. Almost any misfortune can be recast this way as someone's opportunity.

Opportunity theory contains a grain of truth. If there were a God, he might view this world the way the poet John Keats did, as "a vale of soul making." God might see fit to fill the world with challenges, so that by overcoming them we might become the kind of people we ought to be.

No one wants a world without challenges. Such a world would be utterly insipid. Theists might therefore be tempted to cast God in the role of a trainer who keeps challenging his moral athletes on earth with ever more arduous tasks. If the tasks seem painful, that is simply the price we must pay for getting our souls fit enough to enter heaven. By interpreting natural evils in this manner, theists may think that they have solved, at least in part, the infamous problem of evil. They have done nothing of the sort.

Some challenges are desirable; some are not. A sensible trainer might well have his athletes run up mountains to strengthen their legs. Hill work is in fact one of the best methods for accomplishing that goal. But what if a trainer chopped off an athlete's foot? He could explain his action by claiming it made climbing the hill more "challenging." He might even say that the amputation was an "opportunity" for his athlete to practice hopping. Such explanations would not wash; they would only expose the trainer as a lunatic.

Many natural evils are more like amputations than mountains. My father's Alzheimer's was among these; Alzheimer's is, in effect, an amputation of the mind. It caused my father to suffer without producing any noticeable improvement in his moral character. The God described by opportunity theory doesn't seem to know the difference between mountains and amputations. He fills the world with both quite indiscriminately. So while opportunity theory is meant to defend the goodness of God, in the end it just makes it seem as though God must have gone completely mad.

Swinburne would still insist that God had to inflict my father with that horrid disease in order to train other people. Alzheimer's and similar tragic ills are necessary to the production of nobility:

> A world without evils would be a world in which men could show no forgiveness, no compassion, no self-sacrifice. And men without that opportunity are deprived of the opportunity to show themselves at their noblest. For this reason God might well allow some of his creatures to suffer in various ways, since this suffering provides the opportunity for especially noble acts.[xxxvii]

So now the divine trainer's excuse is that he amputates one athlete's foot so that other athletes may tone their upper bodies by carrying their comrade on their shoulders. It still seems diabolical.

No truly noble person would want the sorts of "opportunities" Swinburne's God seems bent on providing. I am sure my brother and I would gladly have forgone our "opportunity" for noble action if it had meant that Dad could live out his days in good health. No doubt there are compassionate research scientists out there who are working on a cure for Alzheimer's right now. Would they not give up their "opportunity" to find a cure in order to live in a world where no such disease had ever existed? In that hypothetical disease-free world, there would still be plenty of interesting work for scientists, and everyone else, to do. Living a meaningful and purposive life does not depend on our constantly battling tragedies. It is certainly noble to battle tragedies when they occur; it is not noble to want tragedies to occur, so that one might battle them. It is even less noble to cause tragedies to occur, so that others may battle them. God, in providing Swinburnian "opportunities" for us, is not acting nobly. He is not displaying the virtue he allegedly wants us to attain. On the contrary— he is behaving in an absolutely disgraceful manner, a manner unbefitting a divine being invested with immense fiduciary responsibility for the creatures he is said to love.

Swinburne would have us believe that noble acts are so important that a good God would have overriding reasons to bring about occasions for their performance. The tremendous value of such acts outweighs, in Swinburne's view, the inevitable cost of making them possible. This is a false characterization of the issue. There is no need here to dispute over costs and benefits. Let noble acts enjoy infinite value, and let virtue be beyond price: even then, the alms given do not justify the deliberate production of poverty; the medical research conducted does not justify causing the innocent to sicken, suffer, and die; and brave deaths in combat do not justify inciting men to war.

While Swinburne's God is eager to create ersatz "opportunities" no sane person would want, he seems indifferent to the creation of real opportunities everyone should want. Think of all the millions of people throughout history who, through no fault of their own, lived all their lives in squalor. Think of the slaves who built the pyramids in Egypt, blacks in the antebellum South, and the impoverished peasants of India and China. Many of those people were born with extraordinary talents for music, art, mathematics, and the natural sciences. Yet they never had the opportunity to become the brilliant painters, composers, theorists, and researchers they deserved to be. How odd that Swinburne's God should think so highly of "opportunities" and so little of opportunities.

Section 4

BAD INCLINATIONS

Theists will blame unjust political systems for the poverty, slavery, and absence of opportunity discussed at the end of section 3. God, they will say, could not have fixed our political systems for us without depriving us of free will. God wants us to do his will freely, not through compulsion. That is why God has to let us stumble along on our own in search of justice. He knows that the blessing of freedom more than compensates for social ills our freedom brings in its wake.

I agree that human beings enjoy a kind of moral freedom, and that this is a good thing. How our freedom absolves God of negligence is unclear. Theists believe God inspired the Bible's human authors to express the profoundest wisdom. They see his handiwork in every letter of that document. No one ever suggests that God's superintendence compromised the freedom or dignity of the human beings who helped him put the Bible together. Why, one wonders, could God not have shown as much interest in the wisdom of our institutions as he did in that of the Good Book? A little divine inspiration granted to pharaohs, kings, presidents, generals, lawmakers, and statesmen at key points in history might have put civilization on a far better path, and much ameliorated the aforementioned injustices. What a sin of omission it was for God not to have aided us when he could.

Humans would stand less in need of God's help if we had a less powerful propensity toward folly and vice. Why then did God create us with such a propensity? In the old days, theologians could say that God made man good. We then fell away from that original perfection through our own choice, and were kicked out of paradise. Today we cannot believe the fable of Adam and Eve. We know that the Bible got the story upside-down: we did not fall from paradise; we rose from apish ancestors. The apes and Australopithecines from whom we are descended probably behaved no better than adult male langurs in India do now. That propensity toward bad behavior continued even as our brains got bigger, and our capacity to harm each other in ever more clever ways expanded. People in the human line have never been any better than they are now. We have always been a mischievous race.

Swinburne thought he had an answer for this. His theory of significant choices was meant to do for moral evils what opportunity theory did for natural evils. The two theories work about equally well:

> Although God could from the start have made humans fitted for Heaven, it is obviously a good thing that they should have the opportunity to choose for themselves whether or not to make themselves fitted for Heaven; and so that he should make them with a character largely unformed but one which they could choose by deliberate action (or negligence) over a period of time, to mold for good or ill.[xxxviii]

Drawing upon an insight from Aristotle, Swinburne points out that we mold our characters by practicing good behavior. He quotes the passage from the *Nichomachean Ethics* where Aristotle says, "We become just by doing just acts, prudent by doing prudent acts, brave by doing brave acts." This seems to explain why we need so many "opportunities" to develop our virtue. Yet our characters do not come entirely unformed; they are not blank slates upon which we may write. God, says Swinburne, created human nature with a taste for wickedness:

> … in order to have a significant choice between what we believe good, and what we believe evil, we must have bad natural inclinations. For to believe something good is already to recognize it as worth doing and so to be inclined to do it, in the absence of contrary inclinations. Those contrary inclinations, of sloth, lust, greed, pride, and such like, with which we are born, give us a significant choice as to whether or not to do the good.[xxxix]

It seems blasphemous to portray God as our corrupter by making him the origin of our evil impulses. When God completed the work of creation in Genesis he passed judgment on what he had done: "God saw all that he had made, and it was very good." We might interpret everything else in Genesis figuratively, but not that line. Genesis 1:31 must have been meant to be taken literally. Human nature, as God created it, would have to be good.

Except that human nature is not good, at least not entirely. We are born burdened by moral ambiguity; the same could be said of our ancestors going back thousands if not millions of years. Swinburne does not see this sad truth as constituting any kind of evidence against theism. Instead he embraces the idea and tries to put a positive spin on it. We are better off this way, he tells us. God did right by endowing us with the urge to do wrong.

The internal logic of Swinburne's argument is impeccable. If life on earth emerged through some process of evolution, then the liability to sin implicit in human nature must have evolved like everything else. It is as much a part of our evolutionary heritage as the shapes of our bones and our ability to learn languages. If there is a God, and if he is both omnipotent and omniscient, then he must have chosen evolution to be his mechanism for creating us, and he must have foreseen how that would turn out. But since God is wise, he must have had a good reason for making us the way we are. And since he is good, he must have thought that our liability to sin would benefit us in some way. Swinburne then identified the only conceivable benefit a liability to sin might have, which would be to produce "opportunities" to make "significant choices." With his faith goggles firmly in place, Swinburne did not notice that the conclusion at which his logic had arrived was absurd.

This absurdity becomes obvious if we ask ourselves a few simple questions. To whom would you prefer to be married, someone who must constantly make "significant choices" about sleeping with other people, or someone who loves you so much that the thought of cheating on you never seriously tempts him or her? Who would make the better second-grade teacher, the man who makes "significant choices" about molesting little boys, or the man who does not? What if your doctor told you that your new-born son suffered from a rare genetic defect. "The sin gene is absent," the doctor says. "There is thus a serious risk that your child will grow up to be thoughtful, industrious, and kind to animals. Fortunately there is a pill that will cure him. One dose and he will grow up with a normal person's proneness toward substance abuse, sexual misconduct, and criminal violence." Would you give your child the pill? Would it not be child abuse if you did? What if you woke up tomorrow with an inclination toward some vice you had never previously experienced. Perhaps you wake up feeling so avaricious that you cannot stop thinking about robbing banks or setting up Ponzi schemes. Would you rejoice at this development, on the grounds that it expanded the range of "significant choices" open to you?

A tyrant bent on slaughtering whole villages would never describe what he planned to do as "genocide." That would make it sound awful. He would have his public relations department come up with a nicer way of putting things. The tyrant's PR manager would then set to work telling everyone that their leader was "right-sizing the civilian population," "engaging in ethic cleansing," or "putting the state on the path to glory." Only an enemy of the state could be opposed to cleanliness, right? But the fact that we can describe horrors with euphemisms does not make the horrors go away.

When I read Swinburne I see him as God's PR man. The phrases he uses—"opportunities," "significant choices," along with "deep responsibility" and "choices of destiny"—are all just pretty words strung together for the sole purpose of numbing our brains. There are many "significant choices" no sane person would ever want to make, and just as many that no compassionate person would foist onto anyone he or she cared about. If there was a God who cared about us, it is inconceivable that he would infect us with "bad natural inclinations." Were God to grant us that false boon, no amount of spin doctoring or verbal trickery could erase the enormity of his action.

Section 5

VIRTUE WORLD

Imagine accompanying Richard Swinburne on a trip to a distant planet where, inexplicably, God did make the inhabitants "fitted for Heaven" from the start. Call that planet "Virtue World." The two of you converse with the philosophers there. What will those philosophers think when Swinburne tries to explain to them how wretched their condition is and how much better we have things on earth? "You chaps consider yourselves happy," Swinburne might pontificate, "since you live in a world with no crime, no war, no hatred or racial prejudice. I am here to tell you that your happiness is an illusion. Don't you get it? You're not making any significant choices! What merit can there be in going to heaven, if getting there comes so easy?" The philosophers of Virtue World would laugh at him. "Poor Richard," they would exclaim, "how foolishly you talk! When you are deciding what to have for dinner, do you ever feel tempted to eat sawdust, or drink bug repellant? Of course you don't. Maybe your decision comes down to whether you want spaghetti with mixed vegetables, or steak and potatoes—both excellent choices. Does the fact that you only desire edible things place any undue constraints upon your freedom of choice? Does it tarnish your enjoyment of the meal? No, on both counts, we are sure. So it is with us in life. We have no more interest in lying, cheating, or robbing, than you do in eating garbage or drinking poison. The actions that please us are all of a more sensible variety. Yet this troubles us not, nor do we feel in any way constrained. There remains lots of work for our practical reason to do, and the choices we make still seem plenty significant to us. As for your question about merit, look at it this way: an ordinary person who takes music lessons may struggle for months just to learn a few elementary tunes. To a child prodigy, things come much easier, but he still has to practice for years to perfect his talent. When it comes to virtue, we are like that prodigy. We are naturally very good at being good, but only over the course of many years and much wisdom-building do we finally become the people we wish to be. You ethically challenged earthlings, on the other hand, are like some tone-deaf person who spends a lifetime fumbling through chopsticks. So we like to think of ourselves as having the edge in the merit department. We are acquainted with the history of your planet, and to be honest, our attitude toward you is one of pity mixed with contempt—pity for the best of your kind, and contempt for the real scoundrels.

"Before you go, we would like to say a final word about those opportunities of yours: you can keep them. Although we admire noble acts as much as anyone, our view is that heroic virtue in the face of tragedy is like auto insurance—good to have; better, if never used. We think one of our poets put it best: *The truly brave prefer peace to courage, and the truly compassionate would sacrifice their compassion to have a world less in need of it.* Everyone here in Virtue World knows that we would fight bravely, were a war ever to occur. We care too much about our comrades to ever turn our backs on them when the chips are down. But why in God's name would we ever want to put that belief to the test? That would be crazy. We are grateful to God that he does not compel us to take such tests. We are puzzled as to why he makes you take them. It cannot be for the reason you state."

Section 6

FREEDOM

If I have read Swinburne correctly, his complaint about Virtue World would be that its inhabitants cannot do evil. Their lack of bad natural inclinations makes it impossible for them to do wicked things, and that is why they have no choice but to do what is right. This lack of choice would then appear to deprive their virtuous actions of merit.

I would describe Virtue World differently. Virtue Worldians *can* do evil, I would say, but they *won't*, because they have no interest in doing it. They can do evil, which is to say, they understand what evil is, and how it would be done; they could as a hypothetical exercise form plans to commit crimes; they have all the physical and intellectual gifts needed to execute such plans. Actually executing them is just something they would never, ever do.

The distinction between "can't" and "won't" is crucial to a compatibilist like myself, who must reconcile his belief in human freedom with his belief that the physical universe is all there is. On this view, the laws of nature govern all events, including human choices. Yet those laws do not force us to do anything. They exert no forces of any kind, because they are not real things existing in the world. They are merely abstract patterns in the way events actually unfold. Consequently, although natural laws can in principle be used to predict what we will do, nothing about them places any undue restriction on what we can do. The range of our options, which is clear to us from personal experience and common sense, remains entirely unaffected by nature's deterministic aspect. This at least begins the process of explaining how libertarianism might fit together with naturalism.

Swinburne, a mind-body dualist roughly along the lines of Plato and Descartes, does not face the compatibilist's problem. That may be why he feels comfortable in asserting that what we do not desire to do, we cannot do. However, our disagreement on this matter is immaterial to the issue at hand. God, as Swinburne admits, has no bad inclinations. He never wants to do wrong. Yet I am sure Swinburne would never dream of supposing that this fact in any way compromised God's merit. Presumably God is the most morally meritorious of beings. Swinburne also holds that God is perfectly free. Thus, were God truly to make us in his image, he would need to make us both morally free and free of bad natural inclinations. So even if we work within Swinburne's own conceptual framework, we still have to wonder why God would choose not to do things that way. Why would God want us to want to do evil? To say that wanting to do evil gives us a "significant choice" between good and evil is no answer. If "having a significant choice between good and evil" entails "wanting to commit crimes and do horrible things to our fellow human beings," then no sane person would want to make choices that were significant in that sense, because no sane person who did not already want to do evil would want to want to do it. Swinburne's attempt to justify God's ways to man still seems not only absurd, but obscene.

Section 7

THE SCALPEL

When all else fails, theists who grapple with the problem of evil play the mystery card. "We do not know why God permits so much evil to exist," they are inclined to say. "Our puny intellects cannot fathom the divine mind. To us, God's reasons present an unsolvable riddle. We are confident, though, that to a perfect God everything makes perfect sense. The best thing we can do is submit humbly and with faith to God's will."

Rabbi Wolpe captured this attitude well in *Why Faith Matters*:

> Do you believe that there is a mystery at the heart of the universe that we will never be able to fully understand, not through lack of effort but because it cannot be understood?[xl]

Wolpe answers this question in the affirmative, adding, a few pages later: "Acceptance of mystery is an act not of resignation but of humility" and "The ability to confess to bafflement struck me as a kind of spiritual triumph, a victory of truth over ego."

"Mysteries," as Wolpe uses the term, do not include those potentially resolvable problems we might leave for future research. He calls those "puzzles." The term "mystery" refers specifically to the permanently intractable oddities, anomalies, and paradoxes we encounter within the network of our beliefs.

Wolpe might be right when he claims that a mystery, in the sense defined, might lie at the bottom of things. Many atheists, including myself, would gladly concede that point. Whether such a mystery exists is thus not what divides the faithful from the skeptical. The key issue, as I see it, is instead this: When a purported mystery stares us in the face, what should we do about it?

Method, as I said earlier, is everything. Wolpe's method of handling mystery stands the proper procedure on its head. He speaks as if the finding and embracing of mysteries were somehow the goal of philosophizing. Mysteries make him feel warm and fuzzy, so when he finds one he thinks he has done something right. Nothing could be further from the truth. Mysteries, like entities, should not be multiplied beyond need. When we stumble onto a mystery, we ought to assume that what generates the appearance of mystery is not some deep cosmic reality but muddles in our thinking. We need to check and recheck every step of our reasoning in order to find out where we went wrong. Mysteries are usually not profundities; more often they are just mistakes, mistakes that we have projected onto the universe for our viewing pleasure.

Occam's razor, first enunciated by the medieval theologian William of Occam, is the epistemological principle that instructs us not to postulate superfluous entities. The parallel principle regarding mysteries has no name. I propose we call it "the scalpel." Excess hair may be shaved off one's skin with a razor; but if one suffers from a malignant tumor, removing it takes a scalpel. Mistakes masquerading as mysteries are more like tumors than beards. They have a way of infiltrating the core of our belief systems and corrupting every subject they touch. To submit to their rule is no spiritual triumph. To seek their eradication does not signal an enlarged ego. Quite the contrary—the humblest thing we can do when faced with a mystery is to admit that we have erred.

Section 8

AMBIGUITY

Ever since Immanuel Kant published *The Critique of Pure Reason* in 1781, the common opinion among philosophers has been that no one can either prove or disprove the existence of God. Philosophers have, in other words, by and large adopted the thesis of evidential ambiguity with respect to theism. Some thinkers welcome the ambiguity. They see it as a blessing. "How lucky we are," they exclaim, "that God has not made his existence any more obvious. There would be no merit in belief, if our intellects were coerced into it by the presence of overwhelming evidence. God has thus wisely put the issue in doubt, in order to leave room for faith." Sometimes even skeptics embrace this alleged ambiguity. First, they gladly join Kant in refuting all of the traditional arguments for theism. Then, in a very un-Kantian move, they announce that since the evidence for theism does not suffice to justify belief, the default position, which is lack of belief, must remain in effect. The skeptics' evidentialism puts belief in God on a par with belief in other unproven entities: sasquatches, unicorns, Santa Claus, the Loch Ness monster, and so on.

The duration, vehemence, and apparent intractability of the God debate has been interpreted by several authors as constituting strong *prima facie* evidence for the truth of the evidential ambiguity thesis. If so many purportedly rational minds distributed over so many centuries have seen the evidence in so many different lights, with no consensus as to what any of it means, is that not itself a kind of evidence, namely, evidence that the evidence both for and against theism is simply ambiguous? I do not believe that to be the case. To think rationally about God is exceedingly difficult. As noted in Essay Two, during the discussion of "The Worst Party Ever," the jury on theism has been tampered with. Our all-too-human fears of death, immorality, and loss of meaning tend to obscure our judgment. Although philosophers like to think that they are more rational than most, we are by no means exempt from ordinary human failings. "The greatest minds," as Descartes noted, "are open to the greatest aberrations," and no more so than when they let their passional natures into the fray. It makes no difference whether our emotions enter the picture with our consent, or despite our best efforts to control them; the result, which is a clouded judgment, is the same. Disputes among philosophers regarding God thus say little about the evidence, and much about the psychology of those engaged in these disputes. From that psychology nothing of a logical nature follows; but it is the logical status of the evidence that matters.

To determine the logical status of the evidence, we must examine that evidence. This I will do over the remainder of Essay Three. I will find that arguments for theism fail, but that three arguments on behalf of the atheistic position succeed. It is therefore possible for us to know, beyond any reasonable doubt, that there is no God.

In the volume *What is Faith?*, Anthony Kenny comments:

> If there is a God, it seems important that one
> should believe that there is; but if there is not,
> is it so important to believe this?[xli]

To Kenny's question, William James would have offered a resounding "No!" Here is what he had to say in *The Sentiment of Rationality*:

> I expect then [at the day of Judgment] to triumph with tenfold glory; but if it should turn out, as indeed it may, that I have spent my days in a fool's paradise, why, better have been the dupe of such a dreamland than the cunning reader of a world like that [the materialist's] which then beyond all doubt unmasks itself to view.[xlii]

This is a shockingly frank confession of philodoxy. James clearly prefers pleasant beliefs to true ones, provided only that the illusions of the former not be exposed until after death. Note, however, the incoherence of supposing that the truth of materialism might be revealed to us after we die. If we materialists are right, then nothing can be discovered *post mortem*, at which time our brains will be rotting in the grave.

I would respond to Kenny in the affirmative. If a question is important, then getting to the right answer is always important too, no matter what the right answer turns out to be. The question "Does God exist?" is certainly an important one. We should want to know the answer, even if the answer does not please us. Discerning the truth in this matter requires that we become the most cunning readers of the world that we can be.

Section 9

THE PROOF

Saint Anselm defined God as "the being greater than which no being can be conceived." He thought this definition guaranteed the reality of the object being defined. God, he claimed, must be conceived of as existing, because if we could conceive of him as not existing we could then conceive of another being even greater than God, namely one who had all of God's other attributes, plus existence. But to conceive of a being greater than God would violate the given definition, and hence involve a contradiction. To avoid the contradiction we must conceive of God as existing; therefore God exists!

Anselm's argument collapses as soon as we distinguish between conceiving and believing. Anselm speaks as if theists and atheists conceive of God differently. Theists, he assumes, conceive of God as existing in reality, while atheists conceive of God as existing only in the mind. This is not true. Theists and atheists share the same God concept. They differ only in their beliefs. Atheists believe the God concept lacks application. Theists believe the concept does apply to something, a very unique something known as "God." So even if Anselm is right, and the idea of existence lurks hidden within the God concept, nothing of substance follows. An atheist may conceive of God as existing, as Anselm insists we must, and yet not believe that his conception applies to reality. Conceiving is not believing.

Anselm offered one version of the ontological argument for the existence of God; there are others. For example, one could define God as "the perfect being" and then argue that existence must be one of his perfections. Kant would say that existence cannot be a perfection because it is not even a predicate. I think he was right about that. However, even if, as an act of logical generosity, we concede that existence is a perfection, this version of the ontological argument will still fail. To define God as "the perfect being" is simply to assert that if some being were perfect, then that being would be God. We cannot go on to infer that any being is perfect. The "if" clause concealed inside the definition may never be satisfied. As with all definitions, the definition of "God" merely instructs us in the use of a word. It tells us how to apply the word, not whether it can be applied. So let existence be a perfection, and let God be as perfect as you please. All we can conclude from this is that nothing nonexistent can be God. Atheists might have conceded that much without any argument.

If any version of the ontological argument could be made to work, then the proposition "God exists" would be a purely logical truth, similar in kind to "2 + 2 = 4" or "all bald men are male." God would exist of necessity, which is to say, he would exist in all possible worlds. This obviously cannot be. God may enjoy absolute power in this world, the one he created, but over merely possible worlds the human imagination reigns supreme. We are free to populate the realm of the merely possible in any manner we choose. It is easy to conceive of a godless world. Atheists do it every day. Philosophers may even conceive of a world where nothing exists: no minds, no matter, no space, and no time. No contradiction results. Let the majesty of God lie beyond all human imagination; God still cannot force himself into that world of pure nothingness, nor into any other merely possible world from which we decide to exclude him.

Although Saint Thomas Aquinas rejected Anselm's proof, he retained a belief in its conclusion. Aquinas saw God as a necessary being. Not only did God's essence logically entail existence; his essence was his existence. For all other beings existence and essence are logically distinct, but God is special, so in his case essence is identical with existence. If we could only gaze upon the essence of God, we would understand not only that God exists, but why he exists, and why he must exist.

We should not let Aquinas dazzle us with the inscrutability of God's essence. How, one might ask, can the essence of a thing also be its existence? No one knows. It is a mystery, a mystery we can readily do without. The fact is God cannot be necessary in the required sense, because, as just explained, he does not exist in all possible worlds. His existence is therefore no logical truth. Consequently his essence cannot explain his existence. This is why all versions of the ontological argument inevitably fail. Other theistic arguments that rely on the concept of a necessary being must suffer the same fate. Necessary beings are an oxymoron. There cannot be any such thing.

Section 10

SIMPLICITY

I think Aquinas fell into the trap discussed in the fifth section of Essay One: he focused on whether it would be good for God to enjoy necessity, while paying insufficient attention to the question, "Does the concept of a necessary being work?" From Aquinas's perspective, it must have seemed obvious both (a) that God could not depend for his existence on anything outside himself, since that would be beneath his dignity, and (b) that a God who contained within himself the reason for his own existence would be far greater than one whose existence was an inexplicable brute fact. Therefore, Aquinas reasoned, it would be exceedingly good if God was a necessary being. That then is what he must be. Had Aquinas looked at the God concept with the eyes of a conceptual engineer, he might have been quicker to realize the incoherence of supposing that anything could pull itself into existence by its own bootstraps. A necessary being, like a perpetual motion machine, is one of those things, and there are many of them, that sound wonderful, but just don't work.

The same thing happens when Aquinas considers the issue of divine simplicity. The most important question for Aquinas is whether simplicity is good for God. He insists that it is. Complexity of being would compromise God's perfection. Complexity would entail having parts. Those parts, no matter how grand, could never display the perfection of the whole that is God. No single part of God could be either omniscient or omnipotent, for example. But if the parts could not be as perfect as the whole, then it would be better if there were no parts. So to maintain the purity of God's perfection, Aquinas thought he needed to postulate a supremely simple deity.

Does the concept of a simple deity work? Aquinas believed that it did. He thought God could easily be the simple cause of an infinite variety of earthly effects. His model was the sun, which produces many different phenomena through its one power of producing light. This argument seems like an afterthought, however, for once Aquinas had decided that God *ought* to be simple, he needed only an excuse to reach the further conclusion that God *could* be simple, and in fact *is* so.

In asserting God's simplicity, Aquinas expressed the consensus view of theologians going at least as far back as Boethius, who wrote in the sixth century. Swinburne and others, writing in our own time, continue this tradition. But what happens when we reexamine the God concept from an engineering perspective? Richard Dawkins took this approach in his 2006 book, *The God Delusion*.

Dawkins is a zoologist, not an engineer. He rose to prominence in the 1970s as a leading advocate of evolutionary theory. Zoologists though, like engineers, develop a keen eye for the relationship between form and function. They have to because animals are even more complex than most machines. Understanding how such complexity could have evolved requires that zoologists ask and answer a host of engineering-style questions. There is no other way to figure out how natural selection operates.

When Dawkins came to write about God, he naturally followed the habits of his profession. To him it seemed virtually self-evident that God could not be simple. Any being capable of doing all that God is thought to do would have to be infinitely complex. Unfortunately, Dawkins does not spell out his reasoning in sufficient detail. Theologians who read *The God Delusion* probably come away convinced that Dawkins just does not "get" theology. "Dawkins is only a scientist. What does he know of God?" one can almost hear those theologians saying. "God is not an animal. Lessons learned from mollusks and wildebeests do not apply to him." Yet Dawkins is right. He has seen something that theologians have studiously avoided seeing for centuries.

To think about God is to reason by analogy. We apply what we learn from experience to things such as God that lie beyond the reach of experience. We need to proceed with caution when we do this. Some analogies are fair, others absurd. For example, we define God as a person. We know from experience that people have thoughts, feelings, beliefs, desires, intentions, and motives. We therefore attribute similar mental states to God. We imagine that God loves us, that he wants us to follow the golden rule, that he intends to reward the faithful in heaven, and so on. Such talk is fair. It is not an historical accident that people just happen to have these sorts of mental states. Such mental states are essential to personhood. One cannot be a person without them. So if God is a person, he must have a mind, and we must be able to describe his mind using the same terms we use to describe human minds. The terms may be meant analogically rather than literally, but they will still apply. But suppose we were to reason as follows: "All the people we know have hands and feet. God is a person, therefore he too must have hands and feet." That would be ridiculous. The possession of hands and feet is not essential to personhood. We possess those appendages because we have bodies; God, lacking a body, would have no need of them. Attributing appendages to God would thus be too anthropomorphic. It would show an inadequate appreciation for the distance between his nature and human nature.

Dawkins's claim that God cannot be simple rests upon analogical reasoning. We know from our experience with both animals and machines that if you want something complicated done, you need something complicated to do it. A Paleolithic hunter who wanted to kill a deer for dinner might have accomplished that goal with a spear. Paleolithic spears were in their own way very sophisticated tools. Thirty thousand years ago they represented state-of-the-art weapons technology. It took trial and error spread over hundreds of generations for our ancestors to perfect their spear-making techniques. Yet a spear consists of just three parts: a wooden shaft, a stone point, and some sinew to tie the point to the shaft. A spear is a relatively simple tool designed to do a relatively simple job. But suppose we want to obliterate an enemy city. Our weapon must be virtually invisible to radar, fast enough to elude enemy defenses, and capable of hitting targets with pinpoint precision, while delivering massive concussive force. A spear will not do. Nothing with just three parts will do. We need a jet-propelled bomber loaded with computerized navigation systems. Our bomber must have thousands of parts. Complexity of function entails complexity of form. This basic principle applies universally, from spears to space ships, and from bacteria to brain surgeons.

Engineering is all about trade-offs. To get one thing we must give up another. If we want to maximize our bomber's speed we might have to reduce its weight, and this could mean loading it with fewer bombs. Payload thus gets sacrificed at the altar of velocity. If we figure out how to retain a heavy payload without any loss of velocity, we will have to pay for that in some other area. The plane might be less maneuverable, or less fuel efficient, or produce a larger radar signature. In engineering, as in economics, there is no free lunch. Everything must be paid for. The principle that links complexity of form to complexity of function is just a special case of that more general law.

Theologians from Boethius on have cobbled together the God concept with no regard for potential costs or trade-offs. They endow their God with the maximum of everything:

knowledge, power, love, etc. This should raise our suspicions. We need to ask if God could really marry perfect simplicity of being with tremendous complexity of action. Aquinas's sun analogy is of no help. The sun does not violate, but rather illustrates, the engineering principles enunciated above. It is a very large yet structurally simple body that does some relatively simple things. It exerts gravitational force; it generates electromagnetic radiation, and that is about all. The sun's form thus matches its function. So reasoning by analogy, we must suppose that God's infinitely greater functionality would have to correspond to a vastly more sophisticated form. For God too, form would match function. He would not violate engineering principles but rather take them to the nth degree. If this hypothesis turns out to be correct, then theologians do have something to learn from mollusks and wildebeests.

Section 11

MAPS

Consider God's omniscience. If God knows all, then the divine mind must be capable of storing an infinite quantity of information. Every fact has to be recorded somehow. God must remember the complete history of every electron in the universe, while enjoying instant recall of every prayer, sin, and saintly deed. All that information has to be stored, processed, and then used to guide the exercise of God's omnipotent power. How does God perform this massive data crunching job?

We could speculate that God spends eternity contemplating a single proposition. This all-encompassing super-thought would contain everything God needs to know. Although this is an entertaining notion, it solves nothing. The super-thought, with its infinite information content, would have to be infinitely complex. So how could it exist in an allegedly simple substance?

Now think about maps. A map stores information about some parcel of real estate. Each point on the map corresponds to a point on the terrain. There are as many map points as terrain points, so in that sense the map and the terrain are equally complex. In another sense the complexity of the map depends on how much information it contains. Each new line or mark on the map adds more information but also makes the map more complicated. As always, there are trade-offs. A simple map will be cheaper to produce and easier to read, but if we want extremely detailed information regarding every hill, river, road, and building, only a very complicated map will do.

A map's representational power depends on the idea that if the terrain were different, the map too would be different, and different in some very specific and systematic way. If a given road were longer, then the corresponding map line would be longer; if a river were wider its corresponding map line would be thicker, and so on. The correspondence between map points and terrain points is thus accompanied by another set of correspondences between possible maps and possible terrains. A map, then, must have potential. There must be at least as many ways to be a map, as there are ways to be a terrain.

The properties of maps just discussed are not accidental. They do not, in other words, depend on the peculiarities of a map's physical embodiment on a sheet of paper. On the contrary, the properties discussed are essential. They would pertain to any information storage system: books, musical scores, computer hard drives, even minds. It matters not whether a mind exists as pure spirit or finds embodiment in a brain. If a mind is going to store information, it must possess potentiality, complexity, and correspondence relations, just like a map.

If God exists, then his mind too must possess these maplike features. The infinite information of his omniscience would necessarily reside in an infinitely complex "map" within the divine memory bank. Features of this spiritual "map" would correspond to features of the world God created. God's potential mental states would systematically correspond to the various possible worlds God chose not to create. God's thoughts about his creation, his reasons for creating one world rather than another, and the moral judgments he makes about saints and sinners— all this information would also have to be stored, processed, and used with the help of that same extraordinarily complex representational power. This is not anthropomorphic, like attributing hands and feet to God; it is just sound analogical reasoning, on par with attributing intentionality to him.

The obvious conclusion is that Thomas Aquinas was wrong. God cannot be simple. He cannot be pure actuality either. The properties of perfect simplicity and pure actuality are not consistent with God's omniscience and super-intelligence. Many traditional conceptions of God are thus incoherent. We cannot immediately infer from this that there is no God, but only that, if there is a God, then he cannot be quite as perfect as some of his admirers might have imagined.

"God has no need of any map; His mind intuits all truths without the correspondences and potentialities you mention," so any theologian might respond. "Then how can those wonderful intuitions possibly occur?" I might ask. "We do not know, and never will," a theologian could continue. "We are not meant to know the details. All we can say is that God works in mysterious ways." But that is no answer, and the appeal to mystery is not well taken. Of course we are not meant to know the details. Yet details there would have to be, and they would need to reside within the substance of an infinitely complicated being.

Section 12

THE UNIVERSE

Although I never had the pleasure of meeting Mortimer Adler, he is the only philosopher mentioned in these pages of whom I can honestly say that I was once in the same room with him. That room was the auditorium of my alma mater, where Adler was a guest lecturer. I heard him speak just once, during my freshman year. At the time I had no idea who he was. I do not recall what he spoke about that evening. I did not become a fan of his until much later, when I began to read some of his many books. I became a fan while at the same time being, in an entirely academic sense, a foe. Although Adler helped start the great books program upon which my college curriculum was based, he took what I consider to be an unduly lopsided view of that program. To read Adler is to come away with the impression that Aristotle and Aquinas were the two great fountains of wisdom in the West and that all other philosophers have been stumbling around in the dark. In *Ten Philosophical Mistakes*, for example, Adler argues that virtually all of the key mistakes made in modern philosophy stem either from a reluctance to read Thomas Aquinas or from insufficient attention being paid to Aristotle. The insights needed to correct the ten mistakes discussed can be found in the works of one or the other of those two sages. "Didn't Aristotle and Aquinas make any mistakes," one wonders? "And are there no original insights to be discovered in Locke, Hume, or Wittgenstein?" Still, Adler's books are models of sobriety and clarity. One has to admire the courage and tenacity with which he championed unpopular views. Certainly it never hurts to be reminded, as he was constantly reminding his readers, that there is wisdom in old books. His motto that philosophy is everybody's business has been an inspiration to me.

In 1980 Adler published a book entitled *How to Think About God*, in which he defended the cosmological argument on behalf of theism. Adler's argument is a modern adaptation of Aquinas's arguments from the *Summa Theologica*. Adler combines elements from the second and third of Aquinas's Five Ways, spells out certain underlying assumptions, fills in missing steps to make the case for God more rigorous, and also frees the Thomistic version of its reliance on the now obsolete notions of medieval physics. Paradoxically, by strengthening the cosmological argument in this manner, Adler weakened it. The greater transparency of his presentation just makes it that much easier for readers to see where the argument goes awry.

Adler's cosmological argument attempts to infer the existence of God from the existence of the universe. The argument does not rely on the universe being inhabited. The universe does not have to be especially well organized either. Attempts to derive an Orderer from the cosmos's impressive order are called design arguments. What a cosmological argument seeks to explain is not order or life or consciousness, but simply existence itself. The claim is that a universe, any universe, even one without people, would require a creator.

Unlike its ontological cousins, a cosmological argument does not try to prove the reality of God with mathematical certainty. Adler stresses the point that even if his argument succeeds, it only demonstrates its thesis with some degree of probability. He adds that a cosmological argument's God is just a Creator; getting to the full-blown personal deity of traditional Western monotheism, the God of Abraham and Moses, requires an extra step. One might take that extra step as a leap of faith, or by engaging in further rational investigation.

Despite the modesty of its goals, Adler's version of the cosmological argument still fails. It fails, furthermore, for the same reasons that doom every version of the argument to failure. If Adler could not make the cosmological argument work, that does not reflect on him but rather on the impossibility of the task he set for himself.

To understand Adler's argument, we must first grasp the distinction between *causa essendi*, or causes of being, and *causa fieri*, or causes of becoming. Causes of becoming are the ordinary efficient causes with which we deal every day. If we say that smoking causes cancer or that a baseball bat caused the dent in someone's car, we are talking about causes of becoming. Causes of being are less familiar. We cannot observe them at work, since they do not produce any phenomena. Their role is rather to prevent objects from prematurely vanishing into nothingness. Think of the stage beneath the feet of a group of actors during a play. The stage does not cause the actors to come into existence. It does not cause them to move left instead of right, or to speak this line as opposed to that one. Yet the stage supports the actors, and without it the play could not continue. Causes of being are to the universe what that stage is to the play. Causes of being are metaphysical, not temporal. A good visualization would be to imagine causes of being operating at right angles to causes of becoming.

Adler identifies two central facts about the universe. First, the universe is logically contingent. It is possible, in other words, for the universe not to exist. Second, everything in the universe appears to be linked by causal chains. On event causes a second, which causes a third, which causes a fourth, and so on. The universe consists of a vast network of causes of becoming.

Suppose for the sake of argument that these chains of cause and effect extend indefinitely into both the past and the future. On this view, the universe had no beginning and will have no end. It does not appear that such a universe needs a Creator. Every event already has a cause, does it not? Yes it does. But, Mortimer Adler, would say, there is still something that demands explanation: why doesn't the universe just vanish? Why does it persist from moment to moment, forever? Since this logically contingent universe of ours could vanish into nothingness, we have to account for why it does not, and that means we have to postulate a sustaining cause of the universe's continued being. Adler justifies this maneuver by invoking the principle of sufficient reason, to which he gives the following expression:

> Everything that exists or happens has a reason
> for its existing or happening either a) in itself,
> or b) in something else.[xliii]

Could the universe contain the reason for its existence in itself? Adler considers this idea, then rejects it. To say that the universe sustains itself is to say that it persists from moment to moment out of inertia. This is not the inertia of modern physics but rather its metaphysical analogue. The physicists' principle of inertia, Adler notes, only covers the persistence of motion and rest. It does not address the issue of existence:

> The physical principle of inertia—the inertia
> that is the property of bodies in motion—
> applies to bodies that have been set in motion.
> When they are set in motion, they continue in
> motion by inertia until counteracting causes
> terminate their motion and bring them to rest.
>   The principle of inertia also applies to
> bodies at rest. They remain indefinitely at rest

> until some influence acting on them sets them
> in motion. They are, in other words, inert until
> caused to move.[xliv]

Despite this difference between them, Adler argues that metaphysical inertia would have to operate in basically the same way physical inertia does. Just as physical inertia allows physical bodies to stay in motion only because they have previously been set in motion by an outside force, so metaphysical inertia would only allow the universe to persist in its existence if the universe had first been brought into existence by something external to it. But since we are assuming that the universe had no beginning, the hypothesis of an initial creative act, as in Genesis, is off the table. In Adler's view this means that metaphysical inertia cannot help us explain why the universe is still here. A beginningless universe, insists Adler, would be incapable of flowing along under its own power. Some transcendent power would have to be responsible for its continuance. That power, the universe's *causa essendi*, must be what we all refer to as God.

Now suppose the universe did have a beginning. Adler thinks this makes proving the existence of God even easier. According to the principle of sufficient reason, a universe with a beginning must have a cause. It obviously cannot cause itself. Therefore something must have created it, and that creative power must have been God.

The conclusion is thus the same whether the universe had a beginning or not. If the universe did have a beginning, God must be invoked as its *causa fieri*, or cause of becoming. If on the other hand the universe had no beginning, we must still postulate a God to be the universe's *causa essendi*, or cause of being.

"Why doesn't God's existence require an explanation," someone might ask? "But it does have an explanation," Adler would say. Like his hero Aquinas, Adler conceived of God as a, or better yet the, necessary being. God contains his *raison d'être* within himself. His existence is therefore, in some sense we cannot fully understand, self-explanatory. Adler hastens to add that God's existence is not logically necessary, because it does not follow from the definition of the word "God." God's existence is, however, metaphysically necessary, because it is inseparable from God's essence. This intimate link between existence and essence, which is present in God but not in his creatures, accounts for why the universe needs a creator, while God does not.

The universe's existence is thus explained by God's existence, and God's existence is explained by God's essence, which in turn is explained by … God's essence. This is thought to bring a satisfactory termination to the explanatory road.

Unfortunately, as we have already seen, the concept of a necessary being is incoherent. Nothing that exists can be either logically or metaphysically necessary in the way that the cosmological argument requires. It is *necessary* that all existing things be entirely *contingent*. It follows that the reason for God's existence cannot lie inside God. Applying Adler's version of the principle of sufficient reason, we must conclude that God's *raison d'être* must come from outside him. God must have a God. By that logic, God's God too must have a God, and so on, ad infinitum. This endless parade of metaphysically deficient deities produces an explanatory disaster fatal to the cosmological argument.

We can stop the infinite regress before it begins by pointing out that Adler has misinterpreted the principle of sufficient reason. Epistemological principles such as the principle of sufficient reason cannot tell what the world is like. We have no *a priori* way of knowing that. The most our epistemological principles can do is provide us with guidance for the conduct of our inquiries. Occam's razor, for example, doesn't place any limit on the number of entities the world might hold. It does not even prohibit the existence of theoretically superfluous entities. It merely suggests that we refrain from the postulation of superfluous entities until such time as they cease to be superfluous. A proper rendering of the principle of sufficient reason will have this same character. It will not insist that everything must have a cause, for how would we know that? Instead it will merely urge us to continue looking for causes. It never hurts to look.

To look for causes is not necessarily to find them. When shorn of its claim to *a priori* metaphysical knowledge, the principle of sufficient reason ceases to provide any grounds for an inference to God. The universe might, for all we know, be all there is. If that is true then, *contra* Adler, the universe does flow along by itself, according to some principle of metaphysical inertia. This does not mean that the universe causes its own persistence. The inertia in question is not a positive power that the universe mysteriously exerts, but only the absence of a certain liability.

Consider this analogy. Sugar cubes are soluble, which means that they are liable to dissolve if placed in a hot cup of coffee or tea. If a given cube failed to dissolve in that situation, we would want to know why. There would have to be an explanation. Some agent must have acted to prevent the dissolution. However, sugar cubes have no special liability for spontaneously catching fire. There is thus no need to postulate an occult agency that might be held responsible for perpetually dowsing these fires. Perhaps it is logically possible for a sugar cube to burst into flames, but that is neither here nor there. Sugar cubes still do not require constant help from any external yet invisible fire retardant.

Similar reasoning applies to the universe. It is indeed logically possible for the universe to suddenly pop out of existence. Yet that is neither here nor there. A mechanism for preventing the universe from vanishing would be required only if the universe had some definite liability to vanish. To the best of our knowledge, no such liability exists. So the best explanation for why the universe does not suddenly vanish is simply that it suffers from no special liability to do so. This eliminates any need to postulate God as the universe's existential prop.

Adler's rejection of metaphysical inertia rests on a faulty understanding of physical inertia. Correctly stated, the principle of physical inertia holds that bodies at rest tend to stay at rest, while bodies in motion tend to stay in motion, unless the operation of forces dictates otherwise. The principle is perfectly symmetrical. It treats motion and rest the same, and both are seen as being equally natural. There is no requirement that moving bodies have been once at rest. Adler inserts such a requirement; in doing so, he destroys the symmetry. If we reinstall the symmetry into both physical and metaphysical inertia, so that being and nonbeing are treated equally, just as motion and rest are, then Adler's objection to metaphysical inertia collapses.

What if the universe had a beginning? Does that guarantee victory for the theists, as Adler imagined? Not at all. It would appear that the universe did have a beginning, which we now call the big bang. But atheists can accept the big bang theory without either postulating a God or sacrificing the elegance and simplicity of their world view. If I am right about this, then God remains a theoretically superfluous entity, so Occam's razor applies.

"Is it not absurd to suppose that the universe just popped into existence out of nothing?" a theist might wonder. Atheists, however, do not have to suppose any such thing. Time, we can say, came into being with the universe. So despite the universe's finite duration, there was never a time when the universe did not exist. And since there was never a time when there was nothing, there was never a time when the universe popped out of nothing. The appearance of absurdity is thus avoided.

"But how can an event as tremendous as the big bang be uncaused," our hypothetical theist might continue. The answer is quite simple: time had no first moment. Consider the set of all real numbers (including fractions) greater than zero, but not greater than one hundred. The set has a largest number, namely one hundred. Yet it has no first or smallest number. Whatever number you choose, and no matter how tiny that number might be, there is always another number smaller still, yet greater than zero. Time could be like that number set. The present would correspond to the number one hundred. The "big bang" would correspond to the positive numbers smaller than some suitably minute figure. On this model, the big bang is not a single event. It is just the name we give to the sequence of events occurring very, very close to the universe's beginning. Each event in that sequence is preceded by, and caused by, other events. There is no first event, so no event is left without a cause.

I will not dogmatically assert that time has this structure. But time could be like what I have described. A postulate to that effect would be theoretically elegant and ontologically parsimonious, far more so than the postulate of a divine Creator who, as demonstrated earlier, would need to be an infinitely complicated fellow.

Here is another possibility. Imagine a set of Cartesian coordinates, with an X and a Y axis intersecting at an origin marked "0, 0." Let there be an S-shaped curve which approaches $Y = 1$ asymptotically in one direction, and $Y = 0$ in the other. Between $X = 1$ and $X = -1$ there is a dramatic drop-off, where the slope of the curve descends from almost $Y = 1$ to almost $Y = 0$. Let the X axis represent time, while the Y axis measures the amount of order in the universe. On this model, time extends infinitely into both the past and the future. The "big bang" is simply that period near $X = -1$ during which the universe began to lose order much more quickly than ever before. Up until that point, the super-dense knot of matter that existed before the big bang was able to maintain itself in a state of near stasis. Gravity, presumably, held it together, until entropy mandated that the orderliness of the knot begins to unravel. The present is marked by the point where the curve intersects the Y axis. When the curve arrives at $X = 1$, the universe has achieved heat death. Its orderliness has fallen to nearly zero. This model provides a different way to reconcile the idea of there being a "big bang" with the idea that there was no first event. Both models preserve the intuitively appealing notion that every event has a cause, without any need to invoke a deity.

Adler's cosmological argument thus fails to justify an inference to God, even if big bang cosmology turns out to be correct. All other versions of the same argument will fail for the same reasons Adler's does. Every one of them has to base its inference to God on a false understanding of the principle of sufficient reason, and they all require a necessary being to avoid the dreaded infinite regress.

Section 13

CLEANTHES

I employed an infinite regress argument in my critique of the cosmological argument. Richard Dawkins uses similar reasoning in his main argument against theism, a technique he learned from David Hume. Infinite regress arguments are thus not new. Unfortunately, their force is sometimes unappreciated by those who misconstrue the arguments' logical structure. An infinite regress argument is not an argument to incoherence. It does not attempt to prove that the hypothesis in question represents a literal impossibility. The point is rather that the hypothesis is untenable because the reasoning that supports it is self-refuting.

One way to understand infinite regress arguments is to see them as *de jure* objections to the hypotheses they refute. The *de facto* issue, concerning the truth or falsity of those hypotheses, is put to one side. Such arguments address instead the *de jure* issue, which has to do with the rationality of believing the hypotheses. The inevitable conclusion is that we ought not to accept the hypotheses because it would be irrational to do so.

Let there be a phenomenon P and a hypothesis H. An infinite regress argument would show that the reasoning which led us to infer H from P would, if it were cogent, also obligate us to infer another hypothesis $H2$ from H. The same reasoning would then justify an inference from $H2$ to $H3$, from $H3$ to $H4$, and so on, *ad infinitum*. Likewise any argument sufficient to thwart the step from H to $H2$, or from $H2$ to $H3$, would do equally well at thwarting the original step from P to H. The advocate of H is thus hoist with her own petard. Any argument she adduces for H serves immediately to overturn H in favor of $H2$; but if she refutes $H2$, her refutation rebounds against her, because the same refutation also undermines H. So while the hypothesis H might possibly be true, it is nonetheless demonstrated to be permanently unreasonable. H is furthermore exposed as an explanatory failure. Whatever problem H was meant to solve is merely recreated one ontological level higher up. The same problem, recurring on this higher level, demands the same solution, which then pushes the problem to the next level in the chain, and so on forever, or until it is realized that the whole process was a mistake from the start. The upshot is this: if we really needed H to explain P, then we would also need $H2$ to explain H, and $H3$ to explain $H2$—we should therefore consider the possibility that P did not stand in so much need of explanation by H as we thought.

Infinite regress arguments directed at theism have the structure just delineated. Their aim is to show, not that God cannot exist, but that, even if he did, we would need to ask the same questions about him that we do about the universe. When God is invoked as a solution to the problem of existence, and to be the unshakeable foundation for all that is, infinite regress arguments reveal the futility of that invocation.

In Hume's *Dialogues Concerning Natural Religion*, the character Cleanthes responds as follows to Philo's use of infinite regress logic:

> You have displayed this argument with great emphasis, replied Cleanthes: You seem not sensible how easy it is to answer it. Even in common life, if I assign a cause for any event, is it any objection, Philo, that I cannot assign

a cause of that cause, and answer every new question which may incessantly be started? And what philosophers could possibly submit to so rigid a rule? philosophers, who confess ultimate causes to be totally unknown; and are sensible, that the most refined principle into which they trace the phenomena, are still to them as inexplicable as these phenomena themselves are to the vulgar. The order and arrangement of nature, the curious adjustment of final causes, the plain use and intention of every part and organ; all these bespeak in the clearest language an intelligent cause or author. The heavens and the earth join in the same testimony: The whole chorus of Nature raises one hymn to the praises of its Creator. You alone, or almost alone, disturb this general harmony. You start abstruse doubts, cavils, and objections: You ask me, what is the cause of this cause? I know not; I care not; that concerns not me. I have found a Deity; and here I stop my inquiry. Let those go farther, who are wiser or more enterprising.[xlv]

Although Cleanthese's speech reflects the sentiments of many theists, it does not address any of the underlying logical issues. Cleanthes speaks as if he could stop the infinite regress whenever he pleased—as if the regress was a passenger ship, and he could just step onto the dock as soon as the ship arrived at some favored port. Atheists could do likewise: "Who created the universe? I know not; I care not. That concerns not me. I have found a universe, and here I stop my inquiry. Let those go farther, who are wiser or more enterprising." But if this attitude is unreasonable when taken by an atheist, what makes it any more reasonable coming from a theist? Here the unstoppable logic of the regress takes its toll, for any answer the theist gives merely provides motive for the next step, and the one after that, and the one after that ...

Section 14

DEFINITIONS

"We can stop the regress immediately," a theist might exclaim, "if we would just remember that God is, by definition, omnipotent. God's omnipotence precludes him from having any equals or superiors, for there cannot be two omnipotent beings, nor can there be any being greater than an omnipotent one. This entails that God has no creator, since God's creator would need to be even greater than God."

The ontological argument erred: it tried to answer a question of existence with a definition that, by its very nature, could only settle questions about a word. The line of reasoning just described makes the same mistake. Defining God as "omnipotent" solves nothing. If we were the offspring of a personal creator, he would seem omnipotent to us, since he could do with us as he pleased. He might also think himself omnipotent, because he could accomplish any purpose he set out to achieve. Yet there would still be no logical barrier to our God having a God of his own. We cannot use a definition to manufacture such a barrier, any more than we can prevent Usain Bolt from ever losing a foot race, merely by defining him as "the world's fastest human."

Were there to exist a God above our God, then our God would only be omnipotent relative to us; he would not be omnipotent *tout court*. Unfortunately for our God, there would be no way for him to tell, simply through the examination of his own nature, whether his omnipotence was merely relative, or absolute. Absolute omnipotence would depend on there being no God higher than himself. Similarly, Usain Bolt cannot determine whether he is, or is not, the world's fastest human just by doing solo time trials at his hometown track. His status as the world's fastest human depends on there being no one out there who is faster. The existence or nonexistence of that faster runner is not something Mr. Bolt could discover through self-examination.

Section 15

DESIGN

Ontological arguments are logical hocus-pocus. They try to pull the rabbit of metaphysical reality out of a hat full of words. Cosmological arguments are castles built on sand. Even if their reasoning were sound, their persuasive power would still be washed away by the doubtfulness of their premises. Although design arguments also fail in the end, they are far more interesting, since they are based upon real insight.

Design arguments have the following logical form: if *P*, then *Q*; *Q*, therefore *P*. If there was a God, then the universe would display order, but there is order. We find it in the operation of physical laws, in the amazing structures of living beings, and in the consciousness of finite rational beings such as ourselves. Such order cannot be an accident; therefore there must be a God. The logical form, though deductively invalid, is perfectly acceptable for inductive reasoning. The premise, moreover, is correct: a universe created by God would be very orderly. God is defined as a person; persons have minds. Minds, themselves ordered entities, are essentially order-producers and order-discoverers. Were God to make a universe, he could hardly avoid putting it in order. Artfully arranging his creation is how God would display his mind. There is no other way for him to manifest his wisdom and intelligence. The human mind, with its powerful bias toward what the philosopher Daniel Dennett called the intentional stance, is thus tempted to see the intentions and purposes of some divinity in every sign of cosmic order. Those who succumb to this temptation are, in a sense, merely doing what their brains are wired to do. It is very natural for us to respond to nature as Cleanthes does, by imagining that the heavens and the earth testify, as with one voice, to the wisdom of God. Design arguments prey upon this all-too-natural impulse.

However, the job of a snarling logician is to expose this appearance of divine harmony as an illusion by continually raising the sorts of doubts, cavils, and objections Cleanthes speaks of. It is not clear how the inference from natural order to a divine orderer is supposed to work. Design arguments take it entirely for granted that order, any order of any kind or degree, implies an orderer. But in the same way that we cannot know *a priori* that every event has a cause, so we cannot know ahead of all investigation whether every ordered phenomenon has an intelligent orderer. Intelligence represents just one kind of order among others. We have no reason to assume that order of all kinds must emerge from the kind that involves intelligence. The claim that order necessarily implies an intelligent orderer is thus false. There is no necessary logical connection between order and intelligence.

Could we establish an empirical link between intelligence and order? One way to go about this would be to observe a very large number of universes. We might then discover that those sporting $> X$ degree of order all have divine creators, while those with $< X$ orderliness typically lack a God. Afterward we could measure the order in our universe, determine if it exceeded or fell short of X, and from thence infer whether a God created us. Unfortunately none of these observations on other universes are feasible. Even if other universes existed, we could not gain access to them. We have only a single universe before us, and with this pitifully small sample size of one, we cannot inductively arrive at any general law connecting order with intelligence. Without that general law at our disposal, there is nothing to warrant the desired inference from natural order to supernatural design.

An advocate of the design argument might try to augment his sample size by regarding the universe as just another physical object, one of many that are open to our examination. "We know from abundant personal experience," this advocate might say, "that order cannot just happen all by itself. Put a few stacks of bricks in an empty lot. Natural forces alone will never arrange them into a house. Let a garden grow wild, and the plants will get jumbled together in the most chaotic fashion. If therefore we find a garden with neatly trimmed bushes arranged in precise geometric shapes, we know beyond all doubt that intelligent beings must have designed it. So it is with our universe. It could not have fallen into its current order without intelligent help, any more than bricks could turn themselves into a house, or plants could be their own gardeners."

This line of theistic reasoning inevitably succumbs to the infinite regress objection described in section 13. If the order in our universe cannot just happen, and so requires an orderer, then by the same token God's order cannot just happen either. There must be a God above him to serve as his creator, and then another God above that one, and so on in an endless series. Clearly the explanatory road must stop somewhere. There must be some order that is ultimate, and that is not causally subordinate to anything higher. Why should not that ultimate order be found in the laws of nature being discovered by modern science?

Natural laws explain how ordered complexity can arise through mindless processes. They explain how protons, electrons, and neutrons can coalesce into atomic and molecular structures; they explain how stars and galaxies form; they explain how advanced organisms can evolve from simpler precursors. They even explain how intelligent thoughts can compose themselves out of the operation of billions of brain cells, even though the cells, considered as individuals, lack any intelligence. Despite the examples provided by the bricks and the garden, matter does organize itself, thanks to these laws. The laws themselves do not necessarily demand any explanation. We need not think of them as having come together by chance, or as having "come together" at all. They just are. They are ultimate—the unexplained explainers. At least we have no good reason to believe otherwise. Evidence for anything above or behind them is lacking. The design argument fails to provide such evidence. It urges us to follow the impulse to see the world as designed, without establishing any grounds for making the inference from order to design.

Section 16

THE DEVIL

There is another objection to the design argument; I call it the devil's rebuttal. Although the devil's rebuttal may seem mean spirited to some, I believe it is logically sound. The rebuttal asserts that all of the order that our universe exhibits can be explained if we postulate a powerful demon as its creator. The demon would be the mirror image of the traditional monotheistic God. He would be omnipotent, omniscient, bodiless, and perfectly free. The only difference between the demon and God would lie in their inclinations: God is presumed to be supremely benevolent, while the demon would be purely malicious. Like God, the demon would wish to produce order. He needs an orderly universe to house his creatures. Why does he need living creatures? Because only they can feel pain. The demon would be especially eager to create rational life forms such as human beings, since our extra intelligence serves to multiply our opportunities for suffering. He would furthermore endow us with the knowledge of good and evil; this is because only morally aware beings can experience the anguish associated with injustice. The demon would thus orchestrate an entire cosmic play for the sake of producing mayhem.

The demon hypothesis appears to leave large quantities of good unaccounted for; demonologists are thus stuck with a problem of good directly parallel to the problem of evil faced by theologians. But why should demonologists not be just as successful in solving the one problem, as theologians are at solving the other? All the techniques available to the theologians are available also to the demonologists. Every element within theistic apologetics will find its counterpart in the rationalizations of the demonologists.

Consider the famous free-will defense. Theologians claim that God cannot eliminate certain evils without compromising man's free will. Similarly may the demonologists claim that in order to produce genuine wickedness in the world, the demon must endow people with metaphysical freedom. People must have a "significant choice" between good and evil, and this entails that some will occasionally do good. A world containing acts of kindness is thus exactly what we should expect from the machinations of an omnipotent demon.

Theologians like to point out that evil is often a precondition for good. One cannot display real courage, for example, unless the threat of death is also real, and so there must be such a thing as death. Demonologists can play the same game. Good, the demonologists might say, is often a necessary precondition for evil. No one could be tempted into sin unless there existed a world full of good things that one might obtain through sinful behavior. Would we ever be greedy, if there was no such thing as wealth, or lustful, if sex was not so incredibly pleasant? Permitting or even creating an abundance of good is thus the price that the demon must pay in order to achieve his wicked ends.

The two hypotheses, the God hypothesis and the demon hypothesis, are logically on all fours with each other. They explain all the same phenomena. They explain away all contrary evidence using the same methods. So if the demon hypotheses seems obviously crazy, the God hypothesis must also be irrational. The isomorphism of the two hypotheses is fatal to theism's plausibility.

Swinburne tried in vain to sweep the demon hypothesis under the rug. A hypothesis's strength, he says, is a function of its explanatory power and its simplicity. Admitting at least tacitly that the two hypotheses in question have equal explanatory power, Swinburne concluded that we should prefer the God hypothesis on the grounds of its superior simplicity. It is simpler, insists Swinburne, to combine power and wisdom, which are good, with moral rectitude, which is also good. Putting goods such as power and wisdom together with malice creates a puzzling dissonance that Swinburne considers more complicated.

The appearance of puzzling dissonance arises only if we insist on looking at matters from a theocentric perspective. From the demonologist's point of view, everything makes perfect sense. The demon's properties enjoy a very definite kind of unity: they consist of all the characteristics needed to produce maximum wickedness. Omnipotence, omniscience, and the like are just the tools pure malice requires to effect its plan for universal hopelessness and despair. The unity of God's properties is no greater. In fact, it is of exactly the same kind, since God's properties consist of all the characteristics needed to produce the ultimate in goodness.

Swinburne would say that unlike God, an omnipotent and omniscient demon could not be entirely free. Omniscience must include a complete knowledge of good and evil. To know what is good is automatically to have a motive to do what is right. A being undisturbed by passions will therefore always do the right thing. If the demon consistently does wrong, it can only be because his mind is disturbed by passion. The passion for wickedness compromises the demon's freedom. He is not free to be completely rational. Although this line of reasoning seems plausible, it merely repeats the mistake of looking at things exclusively from the theocentric point of view. A demonologist would refute Swinburne by noting that the demon's mind works very differently from God's. For the demon, to know what is evil is automatically to have a motive to do what is wrong. From the demon's perspective, rationality produces wicked action. The demon is driven by hate, but this is meant in exactly the same sense in which theologians say God is love. The demon is thus no more disturbed by passion than God.

God is no simpler than the demon. His existence would not explain anything not equally well accounted for by the existence of his evil twin. The theoretical appeal of these rival hypotheses must therefore rise or fall in unison. Nothing really distinguishes them other than mankind's urgent wish that the one be true, the other false. Yet our wishes provide no grounds for belief.

Section 17

THE STANDOFF

To overcome the doubts, cavils, and objections raised thus far, a theist would need to: (a) distinguish properly between order and design; (b) explain how we can tell, in any given case, whether an object is designed or merely orderly; (c) prove that our universe possesses characteristics that identify it not merely as designed but intelligently designed; (d) find a way to break the symmetry between theism and demonism; and finally, (e) argue that God does not possess the characteristics typical of an intelligently designed object. This would remove the grounds for inferring another God above God, and so initiate the infinite regress. Of course, nothing prevents advocates of demonism from performing the same steps. The contest between theist and demon worshipper would then come down to how well each does with step "d," and this would depend on the particulars of our universe.

An atheist can get in this game too. If an atheist performs steps "a" and "b," and can demonstrate that our universe does not exhibit signs of having been intelligently designed, then his case is made. The atheistic argument would have the following form: if P, then Q; but not Q, therefore not P. If there was a God, then the universe would possess the characteristics appropriate to an intelligently designed object; but it does not possess those characteristics, therefore there is no God. The form employed here is deductively valid, so if the atheist correctly identifies the concept of intelligent design, and also gets his facts straight, his argument will be conclusive.

My view is that the seemingly random mix of good and evil in the world generates a permanent standoff between theologians and demonologists. Were the earth like Virtue World, the theologians would win hands-down; were the universe a joyless vale of horrors, then the demonologists would have the victory. Yet neither of these scenarios has played out, so a stalemate appears inevitable. That there are no real demonologists with whom theologians might argue makes no difference. The preponderance of theologians over demonologists only shows that belief in God is more popular than belief in the demon. Greater popularity neither proves nor even suggests greater rationality. However, the outcome of our hypothetical conflict between theology and demonology will be moot if neither side can get past step "c." Unfortunately step "c" does present an insuperable barrier for both. Here, I think, is where the case for atheism shines. The atheistic philosopher triumphs precisely where his supernaturally inclined colleagues flounder.

Section 18

ARTIFACTS

Let us define an "artifact" as an object made for a purpose by an intelligent being. Artifacts display order; their parts, in other words, are arranged to form an identifiable structure. Artifacts also have functions; they perform, or stand ready to perform, the activities most suited to their structures. The function of a baseball bat is to hit baseballs. That is the one thing bats are most suited to do. I can also use a bat as a paperweight, a doorstop, or as firewood. Yet bats are less well suited to those activities, so none of them count among a bat's functions.

Artifacts are not just ordered; they are designed. Briefly stated, an object may be said to have been designed if its function(s) played a causal role in the production of its structure. For a designed object, the function(s) explain the structure. The structure exists so that the function(s) may be performed. Facilitating the performance of the function(s) is, in a very nonarbitrary sense, the structure's purpose. In the case of artifacts, an intelligent designer creates this causal link between function and structure. The designer intends for an object to perform specific functions. She therefore arranges the structure for the purpose of performing those functions. The results of her work are planned; the designer consciously foresees those results before she makes the object. This is how human beings manufacture the artifacts we use every day: automobiles, dish washers, computers, and so on. Presumably it is also how God would make a universe.

Human artifacts are extremely efficient. Every part in one of our machines serves a purpose and contributes to the overall operation of the device. The size, shape, and placement of each part is carefully chosen to achieve the best results. This is true even of artifacts meant to be luxurious or extravagant. Judged by its low gas mileage, a Ferrari may seem rather inefficient. The low mileage, however, is just another engineering trade-off. The designers at Ferrari have sacrificed fuel economy for the sake of power, speed, and eye-catching style.

Even though all artifacts display order and perform functions, we cannot jump immediately to the conclusion that anything displaying order or performing a function must be an artifact. A rainbow displays order. The moon functions to produce tides. It does not necessarily follow that a person must be responsible for these phenomena. The concepts of order and functionality are very general; they apply to artifacts but also to living organisms and even to inorganic phenomena.

The reference to living organisms raises another key point: not all design work has to involve intelligence. The causal link between function and structure that defines the presence of design can come about mindlessly. Darwinian evolutionary theory explains how this is possible.

All the organisms we find on earth are so orderly and so functional that they appear to have been designed. Indeed, as Darwin discovered, they were designed, just not by any intelligent process. To pick only one example: millions of years ago human ancestors had opposable toes—thumbs on the feet, as it were—suited to climbing about in the trees. When our ancestors began spending their lives on the ground, evolution gradually reshaped their feet by bringing the big toes forward. This made walking long distance across the African savanna easier. The reshaping was effected through the mechanisms of natural selection. Walking on the hind legs created selective pressure favoring whatever genes produced benefits for walking. The best walkers had the most children. They passed their good genes for walking on to their children, who passed them to their children. Genes for traits such as forward-pointing toes became the norm because of the connection that existed between that physical structure and the function of long-distance walking. The function thus played a definite and decisive causal role in the emergence of the structure. To the extent that this is true, we are entitled to say, not just that human feet are shaped appropriately for walking but that they are actually designed for the purpose of walking. Yet this purpose is not the purpose of anyone. To use another of Daniel Dennett's phrases, what we have here is a "free-floating rationale" embedded not in a mind but in the unconscious system from which the anatomy of our lower extremities emerged. This is how natural selection always works: it turns unconscious nature into a designer of organisms. It creates purposes without intentions, and it matches forms with functions in ways no one saw coming.

The design concept is thus also very general. We can apply it outside the realm of artifacts to other objects, such as living organisms, which have no apparent creator.

These reflections allow us to arrive at a typology of items within the universe. There are (a) intelligently designed artifacts, such as houses and wristwatches; (b) the mindlessly designed products of Darwinian evolution; (c) orderly or functional yet undesigned entities, such as rainbows; and (d) undesigned, formless, and nonfunctional objects. A rock, picked up at random off the ground, would be an example drawn from the last category.

Given this typology of items within the universe, we may very reasonably ask where the universe itself fits in. To which of our four categories does it belong? The categories appear both mutually exclusive and collectively exhaustive, so logically speaking the universe must fit in somewhere.

Option "d" can be ruled out immediately. Whatever else it might be, the universe is not just a chaotic blob of rocks and gases swirling around in otherwise empty space. It displays order, and that to a very impressive degree, just as the proponents of the design argument have always insisted. We may also disregard option "b." Although option "b" could be true, we have no way to either confirm or disconfirm that hypothesis. Accepting option "b" would require us to postulate a huge number of other universes as the evolutionary precursors to our own. The ontological extravagance of that runs afoul of Occam's razor. The best option for an atheist is thus "c"—the thesis that the universe is ordered but not in any sense designed. On this view, order does not come from design, but design from order. The undesigned order of the universe is fundamental and uncaused; it provides the necessary prerequisite for the emergence of designed order, both the mindlessly designed order of organisms and the intelligently designed order of human productions.

Theists will, of course, prefer option "a." If they are correct, then even organisms and rainbows will be intelligently designed, if only indirectly. This would not invalidate our four-part typology, which could still be used to distinguish objects according to their proximate causes. Ultimately, though, the cause of everything could be traced back to the design plans of God. It would be up to theists to show how to conduct the trace.

We are all very familiar with artifacts. We fill our lives with them by the thousands. We certainly know a toaster when we see one. Archeologists digging at a Neanderthal camp site usually have no problem telling a spear point or a hide scraper from ordinary pieces of unworked stone. So you might think that, with the help of a little analogical reasoning, we could quickly and easily tell whether the universe was an artifact. Yet our intuitions regarding what is designed and what is not, or what is intelligently done and what is not, can betray us. For centuries the world's best minds saw each individual organic species as a product of God's direct handiwork. They were wrong, as Darwin and his successors have proven. We have an innate preference for intelligent design. We tend to see it even where it does not exist. Instead of looking at the universe objectively, we use it as an ink blot, projecting onto it our hopes and fears. To repeat our earlier insight, we are the compromised jury. We should therefore proceed with caution.

Section 19

EFFICIENCY

If there was a God, then the universe would be his artifact, and we could expect the universe to possess the characteristics typical of artifacts. We could expect, in other words, that the universe would have a purpose, that every part of the universe would serve that purpose, and that the purpose would be achieved through the effective and efficient performance of some function or set of functions.

What could the universe's purpose be? The Bible provides the answer:

> For this is what the Lord says—he who created
> the heavens, he is God; he who fashioned and
> made the earth, he founded it; he did not create
> it to be empty, but formed it to be inhabited
> (Isaiah 45:18, New International Version).

Isaiah has to be right; if the universe has any meaning, value, or purpose, it must lie embedded in its living creatures, especially those complex enough to enjoy consciousness, rationality, and the knowledge of good and evil. The poet John Keats was onto something too when he described the world as a "vale of soul making." I have been harshly critical of Richard Swinburne, especially with regard to his so-called solution to the problem of evil; yet he also got something right. If evil were to have any justification, it would have to be found in the contribution evil makes to Keats's process of soul making.

This suggests a test for determining whether the universe is God's artifact. We just need to ask whether the universe is doing an effective job of promoting the flourishing of life within its boundaries, and whether, in the production of noble souls fitted for heaven, it displays the same kind of efficiency as a factory designed to produce automobiles or computer parts.

Several authors, from both the theistic and atheistic camps, have questioned whether God would care anything for efficiency. With infinite resources at his omnipotent disposal, God, they argue, would not have to economize. Must a billionaire pinch pennies? Berkeley took this position:

> We would likewise do well to examine, whether our taxing the waste of seeds and embryos, and accidental destruction of plants and animals, before they come to full maturity, as an imprudence in the Author of Nature, be not the effect of prejudice contracted by our familiarity with impotent and saving mortals. In *man* indeed a thrifty management of those things, which he cannot procure without much pains and industry, may be esteemed *wisdom*. But we must not imagine that the inexplicably fine machine of an animal or vegetable costs the great Creator any more pains or trouble in its production than a pebble does: nothing being more evident, than that an omnipotent spirit can indifferently produce everything by a mere fiat or act of his will. Hence it is plain, that the splendid profusion of natural things should not

> be interpreted weakness or prodigality in the
> Agent who produces them, but rather be looked
> on as an argument of the riches of his power.[xlvi]

Berkeley assumes that humans are forced to strive for efficiency by the poverty implicit in our finitude. He is mistaken. Think of painters such as Rembrandt or Van Gogh. If they made every brush stroke count, is it because they were too poor or too cheap to buy more art supplies? Certainly not. Making every dab of paint on the canvas contribute to the achievement of the artist's goals is just how a painter displays his talent. Likewise with great composers—every note in a symphony is there for a reason. Superfluous notes are left out, not to husband a scarce resource, but because the parsimony augments the beauty of the music. A superfluity of sounds would only create cacophony. Looked at from this perspective, it is inconceivable that God would take less trouble with his universe than a master painter does with his canvas or a classical composer with his score. Surely the riches of God's power would be even more impressive, if God treated each detail of his creation with the same care that any decent author shows for each word in a book. Is this not the God who is supposed to count every hair on our heads? Painters, composers, and writers all love their works. Does God not love his? Yes? How chilling, then, to hear Berkeley describe a God who can so casually bring about the "accidental destruction of plants and animals." "I can always make more," Berkeley's God reasons. Perhaps no one cares if a few plants go by the wayside, but animals have feelings—they suffer—and the accidental destruction nature inflicts on them spreads even to humans. Nature plays no favorites. Berkeley's God thinks life is cheap, since he can make it so easily; his omnipotence has made him the very epitome of reckless indifference. George C. Williams's question should continue ringing in our ears: "Do you still think God is good?"

Section 20

LIFE

Nothing exposes the extreme, and—if there is a God—unfathomable inefficiency of creation any better than what Swinburne referred to as "the evident paucity of organisms throughout the universe." Our solar system sports just one inhabitable planet. The conditions necessary for life are so numerous and so fragile that the vast majority of solar systems probably contain no living beings at all. Let there be a thousand, or even ten thousand, occupied worlds out there somewhere in the vast reaches of space, still they would be almost nothing in comparison to the trillions of barren worlds. If, as Berkeley proclaims, "the inexplicably fine machine of an animal or vegetable" costs God no "more pains or trouble in its production than a pebble does," then why has God chosen to be so profligate in his production of stars, yet so stingy with the gift of life?

God could easily have put dozens, if not hundreds of habitable planets around every star. He could have tuned the laws of physics with that purpose in view, picked the universe's initial conditions differently, even intervened with the occasional miracle—*whatever it took*. The cosmos did not have to start off with all matter exploding outward from a single location; perhaps matter could have begun dispersed, and then coalesced. Entropy does not have to be the universal acid it is now, working tirelessly to corrupt and destroy order wherever order is found. Perhaps entropy could be limited to controlled, localized situations; on the broader scale, a different principle might operate, causing the universe to gradually increase its orderliness. Gravity might work selectively; it could hold our feet to the earth's surface, and keep the earth from sailing too far away from the sun, as it currently does; yet it would not operate planet to planet. If the gravitational pull of one planet could not disturb the orbit of any other planet, this would increase the number of planets capable of being fitted into that narrow band around the sun where conditions would be optimal for the support of life. God could have figured out how to do all this and more, so that the universe might be teeming with trillions of intelligent species. That God did not bother is something of a mystery.

Putting God aside for a moment, we might note that even the omnipotent devil of the demonologist's fancy would have every reason to do as I have been suggesting. The demon loves pain, suffering, tragedy, and misery, and the more of these things there are, the greater becomes his joy. Yet the world's potential for suffering must be proportionate to the number of sentient creatures in it, and to the complexity of their nervous systems. The demon would therefore want to pack as much life into the world as possible. He would strive to maximize the universe's sentience/mass ratio. In any universe he created, the number of suffering creatures per trillion tons of cosmic matter would no doubt be astonishingly high.

Now back to God: can we really imagine that a benevolent deity would show any less zest in the production of laughter, merriment, love, and good fortune than his evil twin would in the production of sorrows?

Section 21

LAWS

The general laws of physics and chemistry are widely regarded as the most potent evidence of a deity, since they represent amazing order in themselves, and are also responsible for generating all the other order that the natural realm exhibits. It is their consistent and universal operation that explains everything from the emergence of galaxies to the origins of the first living cells, and phenomena as diverse as rainbows and photosynthesis. Some commentators have made much of the fact that the equations that scientists use to describe these laws contain numerous constants that appear to be logically independent of one another, and are such that, if any one of them were different by just a few percentage points, life could not exist anywhere. These commentators have thereby inferred that the universe must in some sense have known we were coming and that an intelligence must have fine-tuned the set of constants with our emergence in mind. This inference, however, is very poorly made. Any deity who could fine-tune the laws of nature to make life possible, could just as readily have fine-tuned them to make it abundant. Be that deity nice or nasty, a densely populated universe would always suit his purposes better than the nearly deserted cosmos we seem to have. The laws of nature thus appear inconsistent with the existence of a creator, an impression that only gets reinforced if we consider another, frequently overlooked, feature of those laws.

Objects in the universe exist on different organizational levels. Protons and electrons moving unattached through space operate on a very low level; put those particles in an atom, the level increases; a bacterium represents a higher level; a multicellular creature such as a frog occupies another level even further up the chain. Yet natural laws show little respect for all these various levels. Gravity works on frogs exactly the way it works on electrons. A sugar molecule has the same properties when floating in a test tube that it does when energizing the contractions of a human muscle cell. The laws also care nothing for their consequences in specific situations. The mechanical forces that propel a bullet out of the business end of a rifle will continue to operate with their usual power whether the gun is pointed at a paper target or at a school bus full of children. An asteroid will likewise do whatever the laws of physics demand, careless of whether its trajectory leads it to crash into the surface of the moon or the island of Manhattan. We can sum all this up by saying that every natural law that scientists have so far discovered is context-independent.

Things do not have to be this way. The context-independence of natural law is not a dictate of logic, and hence something that would necessarily be true of any law-abiding world. Context-independence is instead an empirical or logically contingent fact regarding the operation of our universe. It follows that any deity who wished to create a universe would have a choice: he could make his universe operate according to blind mechanisms, as this one does; or he could modify those mechanisms with certain judiciously selected pieces of context-dependent legislation.

Modern high-tech artifacts often come with advanced safety features to make them more user-friendly. Automobiles, for example, have air bags. The introduction of air bags did not eliminate the need for drivers to keep their eyes on the road, but it did reduce fatalities. Does anyone think this was a bad idea? Similarly, many pieces of heavy equipment have sensors that automatically shut the machines off should something get inside or underneath their moving parts. This prevents fingers from being lost and limbs from being crushed. If God cared as much for his creatures as General Motors does for its customers, he could incorporate comparable safety features into his artifact, the universe. What I am calling "context-dependent legislation" would not eliminate the need for mortals to use common sense, but it might ameliorate the worst tragedies brought about by nature's less forgiving laws. Context-dependent legislation could, for example, be used to direct category five hurricanes away from major cities. It could also soften the force of gravity when a school bus full of children falls off a cliff, redirect bullets away from innocent victims, and prevent the genetic mutations that cause birth defects. Such context-dependent legislation could be overdone. We do not necessarily want the world to be as safe as a baby's playpen. Risk is a part of life; dealing with certain risks is presumably how God would want us to employ our intelligence. But I am sure God could use his infinite wisdom to find the right balance. He could figure out how to endow his universe with more user-friendly laws without unduly depriving its inhabitants of any important "opportunities." One thus has to wonder why God did not see fit to enact *any* context-dependent legislation for the universe we occupy.

An honest theologian would have to admit that he does not know the answer to the question just raised, that no one will ever know, and that it really does not make sense for things to be the way they are, and not some other way. He is forced, in other words, to concede that the God hypothesis here creates yet another mystery. An honest demonologist would face a mystery of the same type, since he cannot explain why his malevolent deity did not enact laws causing, for example, hurricanes to aim themselves specifically at major cities. But mysteries are not profundities; they are signs that a mistake has been made in our thinking. One ought to apply the scalpel.

POSSIBLE WORLDS

After patiently reading all of the above, a theist might complain as follows: "Do you want God to create the best of all possible worlds? There is no such thing! To any world, no matter how grand, one can always imagine adding one more good. It is therefore unreasonable for you to require God to incorporate into the universe certain preferred goods that you might have concocted in you imagination."

The funhouse mirror of faith lends an air of plausibility to such arguments. It is the sort of thing theists employ to excuse the behavior of their God. It helps them paper over the chasm between the wonderful being that God is in abstract descriptions, and the very peculiar fellow he becomes in the realm of concrete action. If the best of all possible worlds defense were valid, it would permanently shield the God hypothesis from any kind of criticism, by making that hypothesis unfalsifiable in principle.

But it is not valid. Perhaps there is no "best of all possible worlds." There is no best of all possible doctoral theses either. One can, after all, always imagine a thesis to contain one more insight, or one extra bibliographic entry. That, however, would not excuse a PhD candidate who turned in sloppily written and poorly researched work. There is, by the same logic, no best of all possible automobiles. Would that protect an automobile manufacturer in court, were that manufacturer to be sued for negligently failing to install brakes in its cars?

If God exists then the universe is his artifact, and we may examine it according to the same standards of engineering and artistic excellence we apply when judging products of the human mind. Indeed, those standards ought to be higher, not lower, when applied to the universe, since God faces fewer constraints than human engineers do and has vastly greater resources at his disposal. Unfortunately, the universe does not come off well when exposed to such a critical eye. It looks orderly yet undesigned. The glaring fact that nature's laws contain no context-dependent elements strongly suggests that no intelligence was involved in nature's construction. Any benevolent deity would have shown at least as much intelligence in the design of the universe as was displayed by the inventors of air bags. Any malicious deity would have found a way to turn cities into magnets for tornadoes, hurricanes, and tsunamis. Clearly, though, the universe is neither for us nor against us. If therefore a Creator exists, he must be either inconceivably stupid, or else completely indifferent toward us, and so unworthy of our attention and worship.

Section 23

BAYES'S THEOREM

In *The Existence of God*, Swinburne puts the God hypothesis to the test of reason. He asserts, rightly in my view, that we should judge theism by its simplicity and explanatory power, just as if it were a scientific conception. Pursuant to his theme of scientific reasoning, Swinburne employs Bayes's theorem, a mathematical formula according to which a hypothesis's overall probability is equal to its plausibility relative to background knowledge, multiplied by its evidential support. For the case of God, Swinburne limits background knowledge to *a priori* truths, such as those derived from mathematics or pure logic. This allows his evidence to include all empirically discovered facts about the universe. With these assumptions, it becomes reasonable to equate "evidential support" with "explanatory power," and "plausibility relative to background knowledge" with "theoretical simplicity."

Swinburne takes the traditional theological view that God is very simple. He also defends God's explanatory power. God does seem to explain everything: the existence of the universe, its order and beauty, the existence of living organisms and finite rational beings, and so on. Swinburne intends for these and various other pieces of evidence to constitute a cumulative argument for theism. Just as in a criminal trial the fingerprints, DNA, and eyewitness testimony can combine to convict a defendant, so here, different empirical facts are each supposed to add something to God's probability, so that eventually the God hypothesis is established. Swinburne, though, does not claim to establish that hypothesis beyond any reasonable doubt. He takes the more modest position that God's existence is affirmed by a preponderance of the evidence (as would suffice in a civil trial).

A multitude of difficulties arise with Swinburne's argument. The most glaring but least serious is his overuse of Bayes's theorem. Almost every page of *The Existence of God* is littered with attempts to rephrase argumentative steps in the language of that theorem. I do not believe real scientists ever do anything comparable. It would constitute a most unwanted distraction if they did. The constant reference to hypotheses h, probabilities p, and bits of evidence e leaves the reader with the impression that Swinburne is trying too hard to sound rational. Would a genuinely rational argument for theism need to be cloaked in such heavy mathematical raiment?

We have already given reason for doubting God's simplicity. Nothing that does what God does could be all that simple. Swinburne's conception of simplicity is highly idiosyncratic and seems tailored to suit his conclusion. For example, he insists that infinitude is always simpler than finitude. A God of infinite power, knowledge, and freedom seems simpler to him than anything finite could ever be. Yet parsimony is widely recognized by others as an element within the concept of simplicity. No geologist, upon finding a crater in the desert, would postulate an infinitely large asteroid as the "simplest" explanation for that phenomena. An astronomer, looking at the night sky, would not assume an infinite number of stars to exist; he would postulate only as many as were necessary to account for his observations. Swinburne, though, wants to postulate an infinite and perfect God to explain an apparently finite and imperfect universe. By any ordinary standard, the assumption of an infinitely powerful, infinitely knowledgeable God is hardly parsimonious. On the contrary, it involves the maximum degree of ontological liberality.

The whole point of making our concepts and explanations as simple as possible is to make the world more intelligible to us. We form concepts and construct theories in order to understand things better. One could argue that postulating God defeats rather than promotes this project. If God exists, then he must be something far beyond our capacity to conceive adequately. To us his nature, operations, and thought processes are inscrutable. The tremendous gulf between ourselves and God means that we cannot comprehend him. The God concept may indeed enjoy a kind of elegance and simplicity. We can define the term "God" in a few words, and those words denote properties as intriguing as they are attractive. Yet the fundamental incomprehensibility of God that makes him a plausible object of worship also makes him a very implausible vehicle of rational explanation. We must therefore suspect that whatever simplicity the God concept may appear to have is something of an illusion.

Swinburne contrasts what he takes to be the simplicity of God with the complexity and messiness of the material world. He professes to be puzzled by the odd fact that, for example, electrons everywhere in the universe all possess exactly the same properties and behave in exactly the same way. What a coincidence! To him this cries out for an explanation. But do we not already have one? The universe was not always as complex and messy as it is now. Originally everything was concentrated into a super-dense knot of undifferentiated matter and energy, which then exploded outward in the series of events known as the big bang. The universe's current complexity and messiness is thus explicable in terms of that very simple, very neatly compacted knot. The knot also explains why electrons everywhere are so similar. Just as family members resemble each other when they are all descendants of a single progenitor, so electrons behave alike because they are all descended from the primordial knot.

They inherit their properties from those embedded in that distant ancestor. So if God is not so simple as Swinburne claims, neither is the universe quite as complicated as he insists. The God of natural theology could not be any simpler than the primordial knot of modern physics, for the same reason that Shakespeare could not have been simpler than *Hamlet*. Was Bach's brain not vastly more complicated than any symphony?

If the divine simplicity will not bear the weight Swinburne wishes to put on it, then the case for theism must depend that much more heavily on empirical evidence. Swinburne explicitly compares his own reasoning with that of a detective in a murder investigation. Should a corpse be found with a bullet hole in it, and no gun lying anywhere nearby, a detective would never suppose that the deceased committed suicide or died of natural causes; he would look for a murderer. Likewise, Swinburne argues, we should look for a creative power behind the universe, and find it in God. Swinburne, though, is not entitled to the *a priori* assumption that anything finite and material must have a cause. He must show, *a posteriori*, that the universe has a cause, and that the cause is God.

Some of Swinburne's "evidence" is of no help to him. For example, Swinburne would like to count reports of miracles as providing at least some evidence for the existence of God. It will, of course, be taken as such by those already convinced of Christianity's truth. But in constructing an argument for theism, one ought to abide by the rule of argument mentioned in the second essay, which holds that the evidence offered in favor of a thesis must be better known than the thesis itself. If we knew for a fact that someone in first century Palestine had walked on water and turned water into wine, that would be allowable evidence. Yet we know nothing of the sort. Those and other allegedly miraculous events are at least as open to doubt and controversy as the existence of God. Even the most open-minded of atheists and agnostics will see no reason to take reports of such events at face value. This entirely vitiates the evidential significance of those reports.

Swinburne places great emphasis on religious experiences. But where is the evidence that such experiences put us in contact with a supernatural entity? Swinburne appeals here to the principle of credulity, which holds that we may go by the appearances, unless we have specific grounds for doing otherwise. People who are having experiences deemed religious seem to themselves to be in the presence of God. Should we not then trust that at least some of their experiences are veridical? This appeal to credulity is entirely unsatisfactory, for clearly we do have specific grounds in this case for skepticism.

Consider the sense of sight. There are organs, namely the eyes, that gather information from a reality external to us. The organs then relay that information to the brain for processing and interpretation. If a blind man doubted that other men could see, there are ways for the sighted men to prove their superior cognitive capacity. They and the blind man could, for example, perform experiments to document the sighted men's ability to discover facts about objects at a distance, which the blind man could find out only by touch. Nothing comparable is the case with regard to any alleged religious sense. Religious experiences seem to arise spontaneously in the brain without the benefit of any sensitive organ and without any obvious connection to external reality. Religious experiences do not appear to provide the faithful with any new information of the sort that would prove the superiority of their cognitive systems. Whatever feeble evidence there may be for such superiority is open to much doubt and controversy, and so runs foul of the rule of argument already cited. So while persons of faith may seem to themselves to be experiencing the presence of God, or communicating with him, to independent third-party observers they seem instead to be having experiences akin to dreams, fantasies, hallucinations, or drug-induced ecstasies. Sometimes, too, the faithful are merely putting a religious interpretation on very mundane phenomena.

Many normal people believe that they have become directly acquainted with God. Many people also believe they have seen Bigfoot. If, however, the woods in certain locales are full of sasquatches, then why has no body ever been produced? Why has no one done with sasquatches what Diane Fossey did with gorillas, or Jane Goodall did with chimps? "These beasts are elusive," a Bigfoot enthusiast might say. Really, they are that much smarter than we are that no one can track them down, trap them, or make detailed scientific observations of them? You would think that by now a hunter would have shot one, if only by accident, or else stumbled upon (and salvaged) a corpse. If sasquatches existed, we should expect there to be far more evidence for that than there is. At some point the persistent lack of evidence in favor of sasquatches becomes evidence that such animals are figments of the imagination.

The situation is no different with God. If God existed and was communicating from time to time with mortals, you would think that far more conclusive evidence for that thesis would be available. Surely, at some point in history, God would have communicated to the faithful some little portion of his omniscience. This superhuman knowledge in the hands of mere mortals would be our proof of divine contact. Superhuman knowledge would establish both the cognitive superiority of faith and the comparative blindness of irreligious folk. But once again, all of the alleged "proofs" in this area are quite feeble and open to endless controversy. If after all these centuries of religious belief no better proofs are available, that gives us more than adequate "specific grounds" for doubting the authenticity of religious experiences.

We can evaluate religious experiences from another angle. Suppose a friend told me that he had run a mile recently in eight minutes. I think I should take his word for it; but what if he said he had run the mile in three minutes and thirty seconds? The credulity principle would not help him, for he is claiming to have broken the world record by thirteen seconds. Even I, his friend, should not believe him, and neither will anyone else. To elicit belief in this matter, my friend would have to duplicate his performance in a sanctioned track meet, in front of witnesses, with cameras and electronic timing devices to document his achievement. Although we should always proportion belief to the evidence, it takes more evidence to warrant belief in a great claim than does to authorize acceptance of some trivial or mundane assertion. The claim that someone has spoken to their God is certainly greater than the claim that they have spoken to their postman or the family doctor. An agnostic is thus well within his epistemic rights to ask for some further confirmation before believing that anyone has been personally in touch with our Creator. If such confirmation is not forthcoming, then the testimony of those who have had religious experiences will be useless as evidence. There is no point to putting an expert witness on the stand if the jury can have no assurance of the expert's credentials.

Swinburne repeatedly insists that the burden of proof falls upon the atheist. It is up to the atheist, he says, to prove the unreliability of people's testimony regarding their religious experiences. If atheists cannot meet that burden, then we should accept reports of religious experiences as representing something close to the truth. But this is absurd. No skeptic can prove that no one ever makes contact with the divine; neither can any skeptic prove that there are no sasquatches in the woods, no ghosts in haunted houses, no monsters in Loch Ness, and no UFO aliens circling the earth in their spacecraft. Still, our skeptical antennae should go up when we hear about such things. The principle of credulity does not obligate us to believe all of them, or any of them. It seems virtually self-evident that if anyone claims to have some extraordinary power, for example the power to receive communications from God, or talk to the dead, or move objects with their minds, the onus of proof should not rest with the skeptic to prove them wrong; it is rather on the claimants to show that they do have the power they claim to have. Swinburne himself no doubt accepts the principles just enunciated. He must, for on what other grounds does he withhold belief from reports that God spoke to Mohammed, and passed on to that prophet the wisdom of the Koran? If Swinburne takes a skeptical stance concerning Mohammed, is it because he believes we can disprove the basic tenets of Islam? Whatever grounds Swinburne might offer for rejecting Mohammed's supernatural claims would also suffice to justify anyone else in their skepticism regarding claims of Christians to have met Jesus, to have been visited by the Virgin Mary, or to have received some special inspiration from the Holy Ghost.

The Existence of God offers what purports to be a cumulative argument for theism. It represents by far the best effort of its kind, which is why I have focused so much attention on it. But one of the requirements for constructing a proper cumulative argument is that the different lines of evidence it cites must be logically independent. In a criminal case, for example, the fingerprints, DNA, and eyewitness testimony reinforce each other because there is no purely logical reason why they should all point to the same person. So if they all do point to the defendant, that is damning.

Much of Swinburne's evidence lacks this feature. He wants the existence of the universe to count as evidence for God, and for its order and beauty to count too. Yet the existence of the universe adds nothing to its order and beauty, for to say that the universe is both orderly and beautiful is to assume that a universe does exist. Likewise, nature's operation according to laws adds little to the evidence provided by the existence of complex multicellular organisms, for the existence of such things depends upon a universe sufficiently well behaved to produce them.

Swinburne is perfectly aware of this interdependence; he points to it himself. Yet he fails to draw the obvious conclusion, that his facts do not sum up the way they must in order for his cumulative case to work. Instead, he argues that the existence of organisms only requires the operation of regular laws in those sectors of the universe where organisms are found; it does not entail that the laws of nature must apply universally. But if the operation of natural laws only provides independent confirmation of theism where no organisms are present, I do not see how this bolsters Swinburne's case very much. What good does it do anyone to have regular laws operating unproductively in those barren sectors?

In any genuinely empirical inquiry, it is always possible at least in principle for there to be both evidence for a hypothesis, and also evidence against it. A hypothesis does not even count as scientific unless it is open in this manner to both confirmation and refutation. Swinburne wants many things to count as evidence for theism; what, one might ask, is he willing to accept as refuting it? The answer appears to be: "almost nothing." Theism, Swinburne says, rules out a world in which there is an enormous amount of uncaused suffering. Uncaused suffering is a particular problem in his view, since men can learn so few lessons from it. Yet the word "enormous" gives Swinburne an out. Even if very large amount of uncaused suffering were to occur, he could always insist that the quantity discovered was not enormous enough to discredit theism. Perhaps he could claim that random uncaused suffering taught men how to deal with uncertainty, or that it taught us the virtue of humility. Swinburne concedes that if human beings were unjustly subjected to infinitely intense suffering, or suffering prolonged for an infinite duration, that would rebut theism. The fact that human beings are mortal, and experience only finite pains, thus appears to save theism from any threat of disconfirmation. Swinburne even claims that our mortality is evidence in favor of theism; by letting us die, and so putting an end to our suffering, God displays his mercy.

Swinburne, then, treats God's creation of the universe the same way that he handles God's authorship of the Bible. In both cases he leaves the door to falsification cracked open a tiny bit, at least in theory. In practice, however, he does everything he can to shut that door. Just as contradictions within the Bible, or between the Bible and science, would never in fact be permitted to refute the belief that God authored the Bible, so even very pervasive and numerous evils would never be allowed to falsify the belief that God created the universe. The lengths to which Swinburne is willing to go to save his hypotheses from refutation seem inconsistent with the conduct of a truly empirical and open-minded inquiry. This forces us to suspect that while Swinburne has draped his inquiry into God's existence with the cloak of rationality, it is only done for show, and hence, that there is something fundamentally insincere about the whole process.

One of the hallmarks of a good explanation is its ability to handle detail. Newton's theory of gravity did not just explain why planets move around the sun, rather than vice-versa; it explained why specifically their orbits were elliptical, rather than, say, triangular, square, or perfectly circular. Similarly, Darwinian evolution does not content itself with identifying a cause of speciation; it explains a host of otherwise puzzling details about species, such as why animals on the Galapagos Islands so closely resemble species found on the distant mainland of South America, and why birds possess many of the genes for teeth, even though they neither have nor need teeth.

Now imagine if a prosecutor was to reason thus: "Ladies and gentlemen of the jury, you must vote to convict the defendant. The evidence against him is overwhelming! The defendant is a man, and multiple eyewitnesses report having seen a man flee the scene of the crime. Detectives found fingerprints at the scene; you can see for yourself that the defendant has fingers. Detectives also found shoe prints near the body. A search of the defendant's home proved that the defendant owns not one, but several pairs of shoes ..." Such vague evidence would get that prosecutor laughed out of court.

Much of the evidence that Swinburne presents on behalf of theism is equally vague. Yes, there is a universe, and it functions in a lawful manner. There are men in the world, and also plants and animals. There are stories in circulation regarding various miracles. So? Where is the attention to detail? Where is the great explanatory power?

Swinburne does make an heroic effort to handle the details. He tries to make it appear that the universe we have is just the kind of universe a wise and good God would wish to create. Unfortunately this runs counter to his equally heroic effort to save theism from any real possibility of refutation. Explanatory power and openness to falsification go hand in hand. An astronomer who claims that Newton's theory explains the elliptical orbits of the planets cannot turn around and claim that square or triangular orbits would be equally consistent with that theory. By the same token, a Darwinian cannot claim both that evolutionary theory explains patterns in the global distribution of species, and that opposite distributions would also confirm the theory. We have here another kind of engineering trade-off. To buy explanatory power, one must pay the price in potential falsifiability; protecting a theory from falsification means sacrificing explanatory power.

Swinburne cannot expect his readers to accept that theism explains why human beings have bad natural inclinations, while also having them believe that an absence of such inclinations would display God's wisdom equally well. Now clearly, in arguing that bad natural inclinations are just what we ought to expect, given theism, Swinburne did not intend to suggest that an absence of such inclinations would falsify theism. Does anyone seriously think that the God hypothesis would be refuted if human beings were just too nice? So when Swinburne "solves" the problem of evil, and explains away every other theoretical inconvenience, he inevitably loses most of the explanatory power that constitutes the second of the two pillars upon which his cumulative case is supposed to rest.

In his final chapter Swinburne reluctantly grants the point just made. Theism, he admits, lacks predictive power because "It is compatible with too much. There are too many different possible worlds which a God might bring about." By making the God hypothesis compatible with a great diversity of worlds, Swinburne inadvertently ensures that the hypothesis will fail to explain why we have this world rather than some other. He also ensures that the entity he postulates, and the evidence he cites, will never fit together in the precise manner in which fingers match fingerprints, or specific donors match DNA samples.[xlvii]

This sinks Swinburne's entire case. He goes all in on Bayes's theorem, gambling that the simplicity and explanatory power of theism would carry the day. Yet the God hypothesis enjoys neither simplicity nor explanatory power. Swinburne fails to get the evidence from our finite and imperfect world to fit the concept of an infinite and perfect creator.

Section 24

THREE ARGUMENTS

In several of his works, Antony Flew refers to what he called the Stratonician presumption. Named after Strato, a Greek philosopher of the third century BC, the presumption is one of naturalism. The material world is all that we know to exist, so all explanations should begin and end within its bounds. With regard to gods, goddesses, and all things supernatural, the presumption is agnostic. As Flew describes it, the presumption is a defeasible starting point for inquiry; we may abandon it if proofs of the supernatural are found. The presumption places the burden of proof on the theist, which is proper, for in all situations the onus always falls upon the claimant, not the skeptic. God is not exempt from this general rule of inquiry. However, in section 9 of the first essay, I asserted with some definiteness that there is no God, and I claimed to have discovered rather decisive arguments on behalf of that thesis. This shifts the burden of proof back on me. How, in my view, can we possibly know that God does not exist?

There are three cogent arguments on behalf of atheism. One is the devil's rebuttal. The devil's rebuttal is a *de jure* argument. It maintains not that there could not conceivably be a God, but that we ought not to believe in him, because the God hypothesis is no more rational than the obviously absurd notion that we were created by an omnipotent demon. William James held that we have a right to believe religious propositions whenever they represent live hypotheses for us, and there is no conclusive proof of their falsity. The devil's rebuttal to James is that the theistic hypothesis ought not to be a live one. Our intellectual consciences ought to rebel against the adoption of beliefs that are logically isomorphic with others recognized as irrational, foolish, or downright crazy.

The second argument for atheism is *de facto*, not *de jure*. I will call it the argument from mystery. We have previously seen that the God hypothesis generates a number of mysteries. It will not do to downgrade these mysteries by calling them "difficulties," "questions," or even (to sound very scientific) "anomalies." These are, I believe, permanently irresolvable contradictions embedded within traditional theism, as exemplified by the great religions of the West: Judaism, Christianity, and Islam. Attempts to deal with these contradictions do not produce solutions but only endless excuses and rationalizations. This is a sure sign that the hypothesis in question is simply false. It should go under the scalpel and then be replaced by its contradictory. I do not know exactly how many mysteries theism produces, but I will mention five as examples.

Although God would surely wish to create *a* universe, it is wildly improbable that he would make *this* universe. God would have every reason to make a far more densely populated world, and no reason not to. Whatever meaning, purpose, or value the universe contains must lie within its sentient inhabitants. It is thus nonsensical to create such a prodigious array of galaxies without being equally liberal in the creation of life. For theists, God's decision to make this desert of a universe illustrates God's inscrutable mind at work—to put the matter more bluntly, it is a mystery.

Although God would need to endow his universe with laws compatible with the flourishing of life, we can hardly imagine that he would take no further care of that life. Have not theists always maintained that there is such a thing as providence, through which God displays his love for his creatures? We should thus expect that God would incorporate into his laws features designed to safeguard us from the most harmful consequences of the cosmic machinery. What I earlier described as context-dependent laws would be a helpful and even necessary exhibition of God's mercy. That the universal law books include no such context-dependent items represents a second mystery.

Although God would want to create living organisms, it is absurd to suggest that he would choose the blind mechanisms of natural selection as his vehicle for creating them. Since natural selection is devoid of intelligence and foresight, it cannot design organisms anywhere near as well as God could. This leads to numerous engineering gaffes, and to much unnecessary suffering for God's creatures. Why did God allow evolution to bring forth species, rather than create them himself? No one knows, so this gives us a third mystery.

Although God would, of course, make rational beings, why would he make human beings? Human nature is a mess. We are burdened with all sorts of bad natural inclinations. We tend to act deplorably and to think irrationally. Even when we are doing our best, the talent we display for wisdom and virtue is very limited. Surely God could have done better? Why not make Virtue World instead of this world? Theistic attempts to explain away our tragic proclivity for folly and vice do not succeed. This leaves theism with—you guessed it—a fourth mystery.

Theists have long maintained that God has revealed himself to us through some divinely inspired book—the Bible, perhaps, or the Koran. It makes perfect sense to suppose that God would do something of that sort. Again, he would have every reason to enlighten us with a sample of his wisdom, and no reason not to. Given this, it seems surpassingly odd that neither the Bible nor the Koran contains any truly superhuman wisdom. Both books are very human documents; there is nothing in them that cannot very plausibly be attributed to unaided mortal authors. But had God authored Genesis, for example, he could easily have put into it a far more accurate account both of the origins of the universe and of the emergence of life on earth. He could have told us not just of the history of some otherwise obscure tribe in the Near East, but of the epic saga of the human race. There could be in Genesis details concerning everything from the history of China, to the conquest of Australia by the Aborigines, to the demise of the Neanderthals. Such a wealth of insight, unavailable to humans writing in the Fertile Crescent over two millennia ago, would have put God's definitive signature on that work. That no book marked with such a definitive signature has ever emerged is our fifth and final mystery.

Swinburne asserts that "If God's existence, justice, and intentions became items of evident common knowledge, then man's freedom would in effect be vastly curtailed." If Swinburne were correct, then our fifth mystery would be resolved. Yet his comment ignores the obvious fact that God's existence has been treated as common knowledge in many societies. Did not the bulk of Western Europe's population during the Middle Ages take God's existence for granted, not to be doubted any more than, say, the existence of well-known historical figures such as Aristotle or Moses? Did anyone in medieval times lament that their relative certainty about God's existence had curtailed their freedom? If God had put his mark on the Bible in some far more obvious manner, would anybody today be sorry about it? "In Genesis, God mentions the big bang, Australia, and the eventual building of the Great Wall of China, thus proving to mortals that he exists. Oh, the horror of it all, now that we are no longer free!" Such thinking would be idiotic.[xlviii]

I think Swinburne's meaning is that if God were known with certainty to exist, then it would also be known with certainty that the infinite punishments of hell awaited sinners after their death. This certainty of punishment would in effect coerce people into behaving well, and so deprive them of their moral freedom. But is this true? We certainly know that there is such a thing on earth as government, and that the government employs a police force for the purpose of punishing criminals. If the police were always successful in apprehending murderers, rapists, and thieves, would anyone seriously suggest that liberty had been curtailed? I think not. Living under wise laws, justly enforced, is not any hindrance to freedom; it is rather an important part of what makes us free. Freedom and the rule of law complement each other. By analogy, then, if God's existence and justice were better known, no one would see any reason to complain. On the contrary, we would all view that situation as evidence of God's benevolence.

A variant upon Swinburne's approach would phrase things in terms of faith. God, it might be said, withheld conclusive proof of his existence from us in order to make room for faith. But this is just more rationalization. Were better proofs available, no one would even think of complaining about that. In cases where philosophers thought themselves to be in possession of solid proofs, did any of them ever complain? Did they lament the overabundance of theistic evidence, or wish that they had not discovered those wretched proofs? Did any of them yearn for the days when theistic belief was not being extorted from them by reason? Of course not. Quite the opposite—they were all eager to share their wonderful knowledge with their fellows. For believers, proof is always and everywhere recognized as a good thing. No one ever thinks it bad, unless they are trying to comfort themselves for not having it. It thus remains a deep mystery why God did not confer this harmless good upon our knowledge-craving and wisdom-starved species.

A theory intended to provide a rational explanation for the phenomena cannot survive the proliferation of so many mysteries. When mysteries mount to this extent, a theory is refuted. So if we put the God hypothesis to the tribunal of reason, and do not permit faith to grant it immunity, then any fair jury must convict that hypothesis of falsehood. In a word, there is no God—and no omnipotent demon either, for mysteries multiply with equal celerity, whether we imagine the deity to be naughty or nice.

I call the third and final argument for atheism the argument from artifacts. This line of reasoning also appeared in *The Ladder*, but has been reworked here, and hopefully improved. To recapitulate, the argument from artifacts has the logical form: if *P*, then *Q*; but not *Q*, therefore not *P*. If there was a God, then the universe would be his artifact, and we could expect it to display the features typical of artifacts. In particular, it would be designed to achieve in an efficient manner some purpose that an intelligent and benevolent being would wish to see accomplished. Sadly, the universe is doing nothing of the kind. It is neither an effective nor an efficient mechanism for accomplishing anything. Is the universe meant to be a "vale of soul making," as the poet John Keats so aptly put it? Then why does it make so few souls, relative to its massive size? Why does every solar system not contain multitudes of soul-sustaining planets? Why are the only souls we know about infected with bad natural inclinations? You would think God would want to make better souls than the ones we find here on earth. The explanation traditionally given by theists for the existence of natural evils, such as diseases, is that they are God's way of preparing us for heaven. We learn wisdom, and the habits of virtue, by dealing with the world's troubles. If this is true, then it seems that God has chosen a very poor strategy, for he has been assaulting the human race with tragedies since its inception, yet the pay-off in wisdom and virtue does not appear all that impressive. We are not on the whole a very wise species or an especially virtuous one. The name we have given ourselves, *Homo sapiens*, "man the wise," is nothing more than a self-congratulatory piece of false advertising. The most rational explanation for these facts is that the universe is no one's artifact. It is just a very orderly, and sometimes beautiful, but still undesigned object, such as a rainbow.

CONCLUSION: OF TRUTH

At the beginning of *The Ladder* and again at the start of this volume, I quoted a passage from *The Principles of Human Knowledge*, by George Berkeley:

> I do not think myself any further concerned for the success of what I have written, than as it is agreeable to truth.[xlix]

I believe him. It does not matter that I also think Berkeley got the principles mentioned in his title completely wrong. He still had no reason to say the things he did, except for this one: he was convinced that what he had to say was both true and important. Although Berkeley would not normally be considered a freethinker, he did think freely. He followed the path of rational inquiry where he thought it led, and he judged every proposition that came his way according to the evidence available to him to the best of his considerable ability.

Other philosophers have shared Berkeley's sentiment. Think of Boethius, who wrote *The Consolation of Philosophy* while in prison awaiting torture and execution, or of Hume, who put the finishing touches to *Dialogues Concerning Natural Religion* literally on his death bed. Why else would these men have kept writing to the bitter end, if not from the same love of truth that drove the Irish Bishop?

John Locke took a dimmer view of philosophers' motives. His suspicions in this area are almost Nietzschean:

> There is nobody in the commonwealth of learning who does not profess himself a lover of truth: and there is not a rational creature that would not take it amiss to be thought otherwise of. And yet for all this, one may truly say, that there are very few lovers of truth, for truth's sake, even amongst those who persuade themselves that they are so.[1]

Yet Locke himself provides an excellent counterexample to his own thesis. No one who reads the *Essay Concerning Human Understanding* could possibly think that Locke's concern for truth was anything but genuine. So lovers of truth do exist. I have already named some; there are others. Perhaps they are not quite so rare as Locke thought, despite the great mass of pretenders, of which he was all too painfully aware.

I too would like to believe that my work is both reasonably important and mostly true. If I am right, then I should like to be read by many; otherwise I would just as soon have every word I have written sink quietly into oblivion. The fame any philosopher desires is fame for enlightening others. To be noteworthy for producing sophistry and illusion is the philosopher's nightmare, for it means that we have done harm: we have plucked readers from their cozy holes and lured them to the swampy pits in which we ourselves wallow. What a shame that the world cannot guarantee a proportionality between popularity and verisimilitude. But the world more often takes an opposite tack, by ensuring that illusions will be pleasant, and sophistry well received.

Philosophers set out to be cunning readers of the world. Sometimes we succeed. We take a few intuitive flashes of insight, hammer them into shape with the tools of reason, and, after years of struggle, finally arrive at a world view which is not too terribly far from the truth. Unfortunately, rationality is an elusive virtue. Sometimes we rationalize rather than reason, and make excuses instead of inferences. We then become the dupes of our dreams. When we dress up our dreams in conceptual finery we call it "metaphysics." When we fall too much in love with those dreams, they become our faith.

NOTES

ⁱ Nietzsche quote is from section 8 of the preface to *On the Genealogy of Morals*, 22.

ⁱⁱ Collins's passage appears in George H. Smith's *Atheism, Ayn Rand, and other Heresies*, 156.

ⁱⁱⁱ Scruton's comment about Mackie appears in *Modern Philosophy*, 171.

^{iv} Immanuel Kant, *Critique of Pure Reason*, 373.

^v Kant, *Critique of Pure Reason*, 412.

^{vi} Renee Descartes, *Discourse on Method*, 39.

^{vii} Descartes, *Discourse on Method*, 39.

^{viii} Ibid., 39–40.

^{ix} Arthur Schopenhauer, *Essays and Aphorisms*, 235.

^x Anthony Kenny, from the preface to *The Metaphysics of Mind*, v.

^{xi} Friedrich Nietzsche, *Daybreak*, 97.

^{xii} David Hume, *An Inquiry Concerning Human Understanding*, in *Ten Great Works of Philosophy*, 255.

^{xiii} C. S. Lewis, *Mere Christianity*, 120.

^{xiv} George Berkeley, from the first dialogue in *Three Dialogues between Hylas and Philonous*, 130.

^{xv} Berkeley, *Three Dialogues*, 135.

^{xvi} Epictetus, *The Enchiridion*, 17.

^{xvii} W. K. Clifford, *The Ethics of Belief*, in *An Anthology of Atheism and Rationalism*, 282.

^{xviii} William James, *The Will to Believe*, in *The Will to Believe and Other Essays in Popular Philosophy*, 6.

^{xix} Ibid., 11.

xx   Richard L. Kirkham, *Theories of Truth: A Critical Introduction*, 87–88.

xxi   James, *The Will to Believe*, 31.

xxii   William James, *The Sentiment of Rationality*, in *The Will to Believe and Other Essays in Popular Philosophy*, 97.

xxiii   Dennis McCallum, *Christianity: The Faith that Makes Sense*, 1–2.

xxiv   Ibid., 3–4.

xxv   Arthur Schopenhauer, from the fourth book of *The World as Will and Representation*, section 59, 326.

xxvi   James, *The Will to Believe*, 29–30.

xxvii   The "blank face" comment appears in Wolpe, *Why Faith Matters*, 193.

xxviii Alvin Plantinga, from the preface to *Warranted Christian Belief*, xi.

xxix   The W. V. O. Quine quote appears in the essay *Natural Kinds* in *Ontological Relativity and Other Essays*, 126.

xxx   Plantinga, from chapter twelve of *Warrant and Proper Function*, 219.

xxxi   Steven Pinker, *The Stuff of Thought*, 124.

xxxii   Plantinga's comments on the justified beliefs of lunatics can be found in *Warranted Christian Belief*, 101.

xxxiii Ken Miller, *Finding Darwin's God*, 16.

xxxiv   Ibid., 278.

xxxv   Ibid., 283–4. Miller concedes that he did not come up with the pool analogy on his own. He heard it used once by an unidentified lecturer during his days as a graduate student.

xxxvi   Lewis, *Mere Christianity*, Book II, chapter 3, 52–53.

xxxvii Swinburne, *The Existence of God*, chapter 11, 215.

xxxviii Swinburne, *Revelation: From Metaphor to Analogy*, chapter 5, 70.

xxxix   Ibid., 71.

xl   David Wolpe, *Why Faith Matters*, 10.

xli   Kenny, *What is Faith?*, 32.

xlii   James, *The Sentiment of Rationality*, 96.

xliii   Mortimer Adler, *How to Think About God*, 103.

xliv   Ibid., 142.

xlv   David Hume, *Dialogues Concerning Natural Religion*, part 4, 47–48.

xlvi   Berkeley, *Principles of Human Knowledge*, section 152, 111.

xlvii   Swinburne, *The Existence of God*, 289.

xlviii The Swinburne quote is from *The Existence of God*, chapter 13, 244.

xlix Berkeley, in the preface to *Principles of Human Knowledge*, 35.

l John Locke, *An Essay Concerning Human Understanding*, Book IV, chapter XIX, 697.

BIBLIOGRAPHY

Adler, Mortimer J. *How to Think About God*. Toronto: Bantam Books, 1982.

———. *Ten Philosophical Mistakes*. New York: Collier, 1985.

Aquinas, Thomas. *Selected Writings*. Translated by Ralph McInerny. London: Penguin Classics, 1998.

Berkeley, George. *The Principles of Human Knowledge / Three Dialogues*. London: Penguin, 1988.

Bishop, John. *Believing by Faith: An Essay in the Epistemology and Ethics of Religious Belief*. Oxford: Clarendon, 2007.

Boethius. *The Consolation of Philosophy*. Translated by V. E. Watts. New York: Penguin, 1969.

Clifford, W. K. "The Ethics of Belief," in *An Anthology of Atheism and Rationalism*. Edited by Gordon Stein. Buffalo: Prometheus, 1980.

Dawkins, Richard. *The God Delusion*. London: Bantam, 2006.

Dennett, Daniel C. *Darwin's Dangerous Idea*. New York: Simon and Schuster, 1995.

Descartes, Rene. "Discourse on Method," in *The Rationalists*. Translated by John Veitch. New York: Anchor, 1960.

Epictetus. *The Enchiridion*. Translated by Thomas W. Higginson. New York: Macmillan, 1955.

Flew, Antony. *God: A Critical Inquiry*. La Salle, IL: Open Court, 1984.

———. *An Introduction to Western Philosophy*. New York: Thames and Hudson, 1989.

Hume, David. "Inquiry Concerning Human Understanding," in *Ten Great Works of Philosophy*. Edited by Robert Paul Wolff. New York: Mentor, 1969.

———. *Dialogues Concerning Natural Religion*. Buffalo: Prometheus, 1989.

James, William. *The Will to Believe and Other Essays in Popular Philosophy / Human Immortality*. New York: Dover, 1956.

Kant, Immanuel. *The Critique of Pure Reason*. Translated by J. M. D. MeikleJohn. New York: Barnes and Noble, 2004.

Kenny, Anthony. *The Metaphysics of Mind*. Oxford: Oxford University Press, 1992.

——— *What is Faith?* Oxford: Oxford University Press, 1992.

Kirkham, Richard L. *Theories of Truth: A Critical Introduction*. Boston: MIT Press, 1992.

Kung, Hans. *Does God Exist? An Answer for Today*. Translated by Edward Quinn. New York: Vintage, 1981.

Lewis, C. S. *Mere Christianity*. New York: Collier Books, Macmillan, 1943.

Locke, John. *An Essay Concerning Human Understanding*. Oxford: Oxford University Press, 1975.

McCallum, Dennis. *Christianity: The Faith that Makes Sense*. Wheaton, IL: Tyndale House, 1992.

Marker, Andrew. *The Ladder: Escaping From Plato's Cave*. Bloomington, IL: iUniverse, 2010.

Miller, Kenneth R. *Finding Darwin's God*. New York: HarperCollins, 1999.

Nietzsche, Friedrich. *On the Genealogy of Morals / Ecce Homo*. Translated by Walter Kaufmann. New York: Vintage, 1967.

———. *Daybreak. Thoughts on the Prejudices of Morality*. Translated by R. J. Hollingdale. Cambridge: Cambridge University Press, 1982.

Pascal, Blaise. *Pensees*. Translated by A. J. Krailsheimer. London: Penguin, 1995.

Pinker, Steven. *The Stuff of Thought*. New York: Penguin, 2007.

Plantinga, Alvin. *Warrant and Proper Function*. New York: Oxford University Press, 1993.

―――. *Warranted Christian Belief*. New York: Oxford University Press, 2000.

Quine, W. V. O. *Ontological Relativity and Other Essays*. New York: Columbia University Press, 1969.

Russell, Bertrand. *A History of Western Philosophy*. New York: Simon and Schuster, 1945.

Ryle, Gilbert. *The Concept of Mind*. New York: Barnes and Noble, 1949.

Schopenhauer, Arthur. *The World as Will and Representation*. Translated by E. F. J. Payne. New York: Dover, 1966.

―――. *Essays and Aphorisms*. Translated by R. J. Hollingdale. New York: Penguin, 1970.

Schroeder, Gerald L. *Genesis and the Big Bang: The Discovery of Harmony between Modern Science and the Bible*. New York: Bantam, 1992.

Scruton, Roger. *Modern Philosophy: An Introduction and Survey*. New York: Penguin, 1994.

Smith, George H. *Atheism, Ayn Rand, and Other Heresies*. Buffalo: Prometheus, 1991.

Steele, David Ramsey. *Atheism Explained: From Folly to Philosophy*. Chicago: Open Court, 2008.

Swinburne, Richard. *The Existence of God*. New York: Oxford University Press,1991.

————. *Revelation: From Metaphor to Analogy*. Oxford: Clarendon, 1993.

Wittgenstein, Ludwig. *Philosophical Investigations*. Translated by G. E. M. Anscombe. New York: Macmillan, 1953.

Wolpe, David. *Why Faith Matters*. New York: HarperOne, 2008.